PCP

by Hal Marcovitz

DRUG
EDUCATION
LIBRARY

LUCENT BOOKS

An imprint of Thomson Gale, a part of The Thomson Corporation

THOMSON
──────★──────™
GALE

Detroit • New York • San Francisco • San Diego • New Haven, Conn.
Waterville, Maine • London • Munich

© 2006 Thomson Gale, a part of The Thomson Corporation.

Thomson and Star Logo are trademarks and Gale and Lucent Books are registered trademarks used herein under license.

For more information, contact
Lucent Books
27500 Drake Rd.
Farmington Hills, MI 48331-3535
Or you can visit our Internet site at http://www.gale.com

LIBRARY OF CONGRESS CATALOGING-IN-PUBLICATION DATA

Marcovitz, Hal.
  PCP / by Hal Marcovitz.
    p. cm. — (Drug education library)
  Includes bibliographical references and index.
  ISBN 1-59018-420-3 (hard cover : alk. paper)
  1. Phencyclidine—Juvenile literature. 2. Phencyclidine abuse—Juvenile literature. I. Title. II. Series.
  HV5822.P45M37 2005
  616.86′34—dc22

                                                    2005002154

Printed in the United States of America

Contents

# Foreword

The development of drugs and drug use in America is a cultural paradox. On the one hand, strong, potentially dangerous drugs provide people with relief from numerous physical and psychological ailments. Sedatives like Valium counter the effects of anxiety; steroids treat severe burns, anemia, and some forms of cancer; morphine provides quick pain relief. On the other hand, many drugs (sedatives, steroids, and morphine among them) are consistently misused or abused. Millions of Americans struggle each year with drug addictions that overpower their ability to think and act rationally. Researchers often link drug abuse to criminal activity, traffic accidents, domestic violence, and suicide.

These harmful effects seem obvious today. Newspaper articles, medical papers, and scientific studies have highlighted the myriad problems drugs and drug use can cause. Yet, there was a time when many of the drugs now known to be harmful were actually believed to be beneficial. Cocaine, for example, was once hailed as a great cure, used to treat everything from nausea and weakness to colds and asthma. Developed in Europe during the 1880s, cocaine spread quickly to the United States where manufacturers made it the primary ingredient in such everyday substances as cough medicines, lozenges, and tonics. Likewise, heroin, an opium derivative, became a popular painkiller during the late nineteenth century. Doctors and patients flocked to American drugstores to buy heroin, described as the optimal cure for even the worst coughs and chest pains.

As more people began using these drugs, though, doctors, legislators, and the public at large began to realize that they were more damaging than beneficial. After years of using heroin as a painkiller, for example, patients began asking their doctors for larger and stronger doses. Cocaine users reported dangerous side effects, including hallucinations and wild mood shifts. As a result, the U.S. government initiated more stringent regulation of many powerful and addictive drugs, and in some cases outlawed them entirely.

A drug's legal status is not always indicative of how dangerous it is, however. Some drugs known to have harmful effects can be purchased legally in the United States and elsewhere. Nicotine, a key ingredient in cigarettes, is known to be highly addictive. In an effort to meet their bodies' demands for nicotine, smokers expose themselves to lung cancer, emphysema, and other life-threatening conditions. Despite these risks, nicotine is legal almost everywhere.

Other drugs that cannot be purchased or sold legally are the subject of much debate regarding their effects on physical and mental health. Marijuana, sometimes described as a gateway drug that leads users to other drugs, cannot legally be used, grown, or sold in this country. However, some research suggests that marijuana is neither addictive nor a gateway drug and that it might actually benefit cancer and AIDS patients by reducing pain and encouraging failing appetites. Despite these findings and occasional legislative attempts to change the drug's status, marijuana remains illegal.

The Drug Education Library examines the paradox of drugs and drug use in America by focusing on some of the most commonly used and abused drugs or categories of drugs available today. By discussing objectively the many types of drugs, their intended purposes, their effects (both planned and unplanned), and the controversies surrounding them, the books in this series provide readers with an understanding of the complex role drugs and drug use play in American society. Informative sidebars, annotated bibliographies, and organizations to contact lists highlight the text and provide young readers with many opportunities for further discussion and research.

Introduction

PCP:
An American
Tragedy

Some drugs, like cocaine and opium, have histories that date back centuries. Their stories originate in dense tropical rain forests or remote corners of Asia, where the use of these drugs was acceptable in some ancient cultures. However, no such exotic history surrounds the drug phencyclidine, also known as PCP. This drug is manufactured in underground labs, using chemicals available on the open market. PCP was originally developed in the 1950s with the hope that it would be a wonder anesthesia and painkiller, but the drug was soon discarded because patients exhibited bizarre side effects that included hallucinations and delusional behavior. Still, it did not take long for PCP to find its way onto the illegal drug market.

People are attracted to PCP for many reasons. The drug is inexpensive: on some city streets in the United States, it can be bought for as little as five dollars a dose. It acts quickly: the user will feel the effects of the drug within minutes. And it delivers a high unlike any other drug: physically, its user will feel a numbness and resilience to pain; mentally, the user can experience extreme paranoia. Additionally, PCP users often dissociate from reality, meaning they lose touch with the real world. Some feel threatened and panicky, while others may become fearless. People under the influence of phencyclidine have subjected themselves to serious injuries or committed terrible, violent crimes.

PCP users who manage to stay out of jail or mental institutions usually wind up in drug treatment programs. Often, it takes them a decade or more to overcome their addictions. In the meantime, the users pay a great price for their habits. They face long-lasting health problems that include depression, memory loss, speech difficulties, weight loss, reduced blood pressure, respiratory problems, and kidney failure. Babies born to women who used PCP while they were pregnant often suffer developmental disabilities that cause them to be slow learners or physically handicapped.

PCP appeals to young people in part because the drug is so cheap. According to *Monitoring the Future*, the University of Michigan's annual study of drug abuse among young people, about 2.5 percent of American high school seniors experimented

In some U.S. cities, PCP can be purchased for as little as five dollars a dose.

with PCP in 2003. That figure is well below the number of students who use marijuana or experiment with cocaine or ecstasy, but it is higher than the number of students who try heroin.

Other information also indicates increased PCP use in recent years. In Prince George's County, Maryland, for example, the county's police laboratory received more than 115 PCP samples for testing in 2002. Just two years before, the lab had received a mere eight samples. "It was a pretty phenomenal change," said Christopher Wuerker, an emergency room physician at the nearby Washington Hospital Center. "It seemed to go from a drug that was out there and you'd see it occasionally, to seeing it constantly."[1]

In 2003, after a New York City man convicted in the murders of four people was found to be under the influence of PCP, the *New York Times* reported that "the federal Drug Enforcement Administration [DEA] has noted that PCP abuse, once displaced by crack, is 'increasing slightly' nationwide. But New York re-

PCP is often ingested in conjunction with other drugs, such as marijuana (pictured below) or ordinary cigarettes.

searchers said that there is little statistical proof of a comeback, in part because PCP makes up a tiny fraction of illegal drugs used."[2] That statement prompted an epidemiologist of the New York Academy of Medicine and a director of the academy to write a letter to the newspaper, wherein they explained that they had reached a far different conclusion about PCP than had been reported in the paper. They cited studies by their organization that found PCP use becoming increasingly widespread. Their letter warned: "Among 199 drug users recruited in 1997–98, 5.8 percent reported using PCP at least once in the past six months. Among 605 drug users recruited between 2002 and 2003, 15.2 percent reported using PCP in the prior six months. This increase in PCP use in New York City warrants further consideration."[3]

Unique Place in the Drug Culture

PCP occupies a unique place in the American drug culture, and it is largely a problem for Americans. The drug is manufactured in the United States in large quantities, and there is little known importation of phencyclidine from other countries. Occasionally, U.S. customs agents working on the Mexican border will uncover a batch of PCP heading for the United States, but authorities believe the amount of phencyclidine imported from Latin America is tiny when compared to the quantities of cocaine and marijuana that are shipped north.

Nor is there believed to be widespread exportation of the drug from the United States to foreign lands or widespread manufacturing and use of the drug in other countries. For instance, drug authorities in Europe and other parts of the world say abuse of PCP is rare in their communities. In Canada, law enforcement agencies have uncovered PCP labs operating in some of the nation's big cities; nevertheless, drug authorities report that the so-called synthetic drugs, including PCP, "continue to be available in the Canadian illicit market in small to moderate quantities."[4]

And so PCP is a problem known mostly by Americans. But how has the United States responded to the crisis? Perhaps not on the scale deserved. In March 2004, DEA Administrator Karen P.

Tandy testified before the U.S. House Appropriations Committee, outlining her agency's goals in the overall drug war. She presented a fifteen-thousand-word statement to the congressional committee, which oversees her agency's $1.8 billion budget. Tandy never mentioned the word "phencyclidine" during her lengthy testimony. Instead, she concentrated on her agency's efforts to stem cocaine, heroin, and marijuana imports, some of which help finance the activities of foreign terrorists, and to address the abuse in the United States of oxycodone, a prescription painkiller that has recently become a hot commodity on the illegal drug market.

Certainly, PCP is not neglected by drug agencies. The DEA as well as state and local police departments continually report successful raids on illegal PCP labs. Nevertheless, PCP has become a national tragedy that is sorely in need of a national strategy.

 # Chapter 1

Good Intentions Go Awry

For Dr. Victor Maddox and Dr. Graham Chen, it was a noble quest: development of a safe and effective anesthetic that could be administered to patients undergoing serious and painful surgeries. Maddox and Chen were chemists working in the product development division of Parke-Davis and Company, a major pharmaceutical firm headquartered in Detroit, Michigan. The two men had no idea that their discovery of a new drug would have serious ramifications. In the decades that followed their work, PCP abuse would grow into a national tragedy, ensnaring many of its victims in lives afflicted with substance abuse and mental illness. More than twenty years after their experiments, drug researcher Harvey W. Feldman wrote, "Probably no drug, not even heroin, which for fifty years has been considered the ultimate monster drug, has been considered more dangerous by drug abuse experts than PCP."[5]

At First, a Major Breakthrough

For centuries, doctors had been forced to perform surgeries such as amputations, appendix removals, or even common tooth extractions without anesthesia, but by the nineteenth century physicians

11

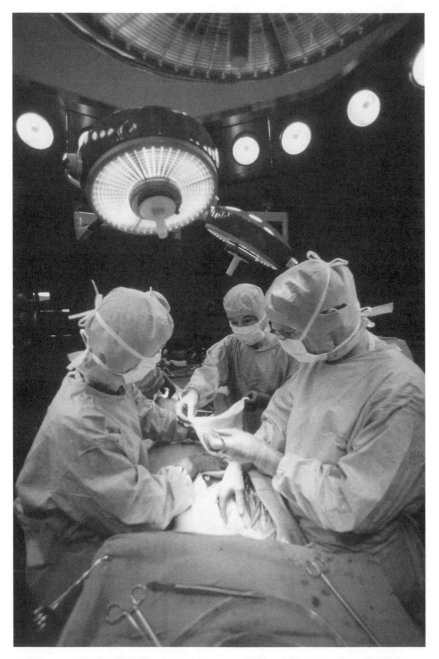

PCP was developed in the 1950s for use as an anesthetic during surgery.

were experimenting with a number of chemical agents that put their patients to sleep. Strong drugs such as ether and chloroform proved to be effective, but their serious side effects—liver and kidney damage, nausea, vomiting, and even sudden death—led scientists to keep looking for other answers.

A Promising Discovery

Working at Parke-Davis in 1956, Maddox and Chen believed they found a promising anesthetic when they developed a compound known as 1-phenyl-cyclohexylpiperidine, or, as it became more commonly known, phencyclidine or PCP. There had been experiments with PCP-like compounds dating back to the 1920s, but it was during the 1950s, in the laboratories headed by Maddox and Chen, when experiments on animals suggested that phencyclidine could be effective in safely putting patients to sleep before their surgeries and in deadening their pain afterward. A problem with many anesthetics in use at the time was their high "therapeutic ratios," meaning that fairly low doses of the compounds could be hazardous to patients. Indeed, most commonly used anesthetics of the era had a therapeutic ratio of two. In other words, a fatal dose equated to just twice the amount of the anesthetic needed to put a patient to sleep. In the case of phencyclidine, however, Maddox and Chen found a much less hazardous therapeutic ratio of twenty-six. This meant that the amount of PCP that would kill a patient was much more than the amount needed to safely sedate the patient, making the risk of an accidental fatal overdose less likely.

PCP had other advantages as well. Unlike other anesthetics used at the time, phencyclidine had no apparent effect on the patient's brain and central nervous system, always a concern during surgery. Patients undergoing surgeries while anesthetized with PCP maintained steady, even normal, pulse rates. In light of these advantages, development of phencyclidine was regarded as a major breakthrough. Parke-Davis received a patent for the compound under the brand name Sernyl, a term derived from the word "serene." At that point, the company received permission from the U.S. Food and Drug Administration to experiment with Sernyl on human subjects. Some three thousand volunteers, many of them college students or prison inmates, were eventually anesthetized with Sernyl.

Disturbing Side Effects

As the drug was tested during the next few years, many of the patients who took phencyclidine started exhibiting unusual and bizarre side effects, such as delirium, paranoia, and feelings of terror. Some patients developed schizophrenic behaviors, meaning they harbored a distorted view of reality while experiencing delusions and hallucinations. Some patients became violent, while others slipped into coma-like trances. While many anesthetics cause patients to have little or no memories of their surgeries, with Sernyl some patients developed amnesia that lasted unusually long periods of time. "While postoperative amnesia is common to all anesthetics, the state produced by Sernyl was found to persist for as long as 24 hours in some patients," wrote drug abuse researchers George M. Beschner and Harvey W. Feldman in a 1979 study on the effects of PCP. "Although most patients experienced no adverse consequences and awoke from their unconsciousness free of pain and mildly euphoric, others had a prolonged and unexplained recovery period of several weeks, marked by semiconsciousness and disorientation."[6] Many patients also developed slurred speech, nightmares, and personality swings. Usually, the side effects wore off after three to five days, although in some cases the side effects lingered a week or more.

Phencyclidine was classified as a type of drug called a hallucinogen. People who take hallucinogens often dissociate: their perceptions of reality are distorted; they see images, hear sounds, and feel sensations that seem real but do not exist. In 1965 the Food and Drug Administration ruled that Sernyl could not be used as a human anesthetic. "Because other modern anesthetics were more adaptable to the modern technology of the hospital, there was little medical interest in pursuing further legitimate uses of phencyclidine,"[7] wrote Beschner and Feldman. In fact, the only legitimate use of Sernyl appeared to be as an anesthetic for animals, so experiments continued in this arena. It was still believed that phencyclidine could be useful to veterinarians as a tranquilizer for horses.

It did not take long for phencyclidine to find its way onto the streets. During the 1960s, many young people started experimenting with illegal drugs. Marijuana use was common, to be sure, but young people were also trying harder drugs—the hallucinogen LSD, for example, along with heroin, hashish, barbiturates, and methamphetamines. By 1967, the Haight-Ashbury district of San Francisco had become the unofficial headquarters of the hippie movement. Thousands of young people flocked to the neighborhood to escape the authority of their parents and to experiment with the many drugs that were freely available on the streets. Many of those young people suffered bad experiences

The side effects of PCP, such as hallucinations and schizophrenic behavior, led the FDA to ban the drug in 1965.

The first cases of people suffering from the effects of PCP were treated at the Haight Ashbury Free Medical Clinic during 1967.

("bad trips") and overdoses and made their way to the Haight-Ashbury Free Medical Clinic for treatment. It was at the Free Clinic in 1967 that doctors first started treating young patients for the effects of PCP.

On the street, the drug was known as the PeaCe Pill—a nickname taken from the initials PCP. At first, the Free Clinic doctors thought the young, delusional patients they were seeing were the victims of a bad batch of LSD, but lab tests on sample PeaCe Pills confiscated at the clinic confirmed the drug's main ingredient—phencyclidine. Doctors at the Free Clinic saw patients under the influence of PCP exhibit bizarre, unpredictable, and often violent behavior. However, they were convinced that phencyclidine would have a short life as a street drug, believing that their hippie clientele preferred the much more mellow experiences one could expect from marijuana or the colorful, mind-altering trips LSD was known to provide.

The doctors could not have been more wrong. By the 1970s, phencyclidine was a very commonly used illegal drug, readily available on city streets and in suburban schoolyards. Describing PCP users, Free Clinic pharmacist Greg Hayner told a news reporter: "People get very paranoid and combative. They think what they're experiencing is reality and they react like their very lives are dependent on it, so they are liable to hurt themselves or those around them."[8]

Caught up in the Frenzy

As with most illegal drugs, it has always been difficult to truly know how many people use PCP. One way law enforcement and human services agencies track illegal drug use is through the Drug Abuse Warning Network (DAWN) which compiles statistics on the number of people treated in hospital emergency rooms for overdoses and similar drug-related emergencies. In 1972, DAWN reported that phencyclidine was a little known and little-abused drug, at least with regard to the number of people treated in emergency rooms for PCP abuse. That year, DAWN ranked PCP as the twenty-third most abused drug in America. Two years later, DAWN reported that in the 662 hospital emergency rooms participating in its network, a mere 54 patients had been treated for phencyclidine abuse. At the time, it hardly seemed that PCP was a growing threat, but phencyclidine's lowly place on the drug abuse scale would soon change.

In 1976, DAWN reported 111 emergency room treatments of PCP users. In 1977, hospital emergency rooms reported 30 PCP-related deaths, nearly double the number reported the previous year. Certainly, those numbers were still quite insignificant compared to the thousands of overdoses a year attributed to heroin, speed, LSD, and other drugs, but experts started suspecting that the problem of phencyclidine abuse actually was more widespread than the statistics indicated. Commenting on the number of PCP-related fatalities reported by DAWN in 1977, a National Institute on Drug Abuse study warned that "such figures are likely to be minimal estimates of the actual extent of PCP-related mortality."[9]

High-School Students Discover PCP
By the end of the 1970s, DAWN reported that phencyclidine had become the fifth most abused drug in the United States. By then, it had been introduced to a young market. In 1979, the National Institute on Drug Abuse reported that 7 percent of all high school seniors had experimented with phencyclidine. One study reported that it was not unusual for high school students to use PCP while in school. Researcher James M. Walters, who studied PCP use by high school students in Philadelphia, wrote, "For many teenagers, partying begins shortly after waking up in the morning, when they smoke their first 'joint' [or marijuana cigarette]. Although few of them go to high school high on PCP, most do show up there already 'high.' From then on through the school day, in the bathrooms between classes or on the lawn during lunch and study periods, friends meet to share a joint or 'do a line of buzz' (snort PCP)." Walters spoke with one student named Patty, who told him, "You can always tell who's straight in school; they're the ones walking slow down the hallways. Anybody that's cool is runnin' to the bathroom to smoke."

"By the end of each day," Walters added, "in fact, usually by the end of lunch, huge numbers of students are too high even to participate in the classroom. One teacher bitterly admitted that faculty vie for the morning class periods since 'most of the students are hopelessly stoned after lunch.'"[10]

Many high school students were also experimenting with PCP at rock concerts—places where drugs flow freely through the crowd and where young people, caught up in the frenzy of the moment, are known to ingest substances without asking what they are made of. "The rock concert is the environment for one of the most popular and spectacular 'rituals of controlled drug use,'" according to the introduction to a 1982 study on drug use at concerts, written by Free Clinic staff members John A. Newmeyer and Gregory L. Johnson. "By charting patterns of drug use at

Special K

There are more than thirty drugs whose chemical compositions, or analogs, are similar to that of phencyclidine. One of the most common, and most abused, of these PCP analogs is ketamine. On the street, ketamine is known as "Special K."

Like PCP, ketamine is a dissociative hallucinogen. It is available in liquid, powder, or pill form, although it is most commonly distributed as a powder that can be sprinkled on marijuana or tobacco or inhaled through the nose like cocaine. Unlike PCP, ketamine is a legal drug in the United States; health care professionals administer it as an anesthetic and painkiller to both humans and animals. In the U.S., it cannot be obtained without a prescription.

Ketamine is rarely cooked in illegal basement labs because under such conditions it is much more difficult to make than PCP. Most ketamine is stolen from veterinary offices or imported from Mexico, where it can be found in pharmacies and is available without a prescription.

Originally, ketamine was developed as an alternative to PCP; it was hoped that it could be an effective painkiller, with none of phencyclidine's violent and unpredictable aftereffects. In fact, when used in doses approved by physicians, ketamine is an effective anesthetic. When abused, though, the drug causes a number of reactions that range from pleasant, floating feelings to chaotic, terrifying episodes to complete detachment from one's senses. Experiencing a bad trip on ketamine is known as "falling into the K-hole."

Unlike PCP, which has a bitter taste, ketamine is odorless and tasteless. These characteristics have led to its use as a date-rape drug. Victims of date rape have reported being on a date and ingesting the drug unknowingly after it was slipped into their food or drinks; these women were made vulnerable by the drug and then were raped.

Ketamine is a drug that is chemically similar to PCP.

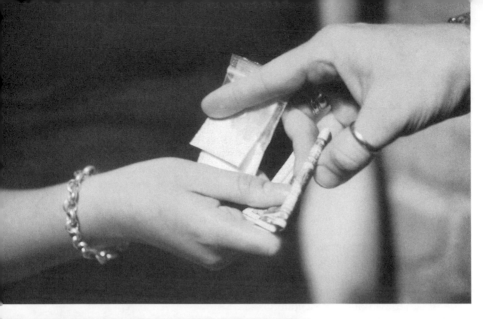

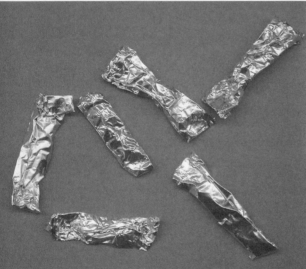

PCP is commonly sold as a powder, known as Angel Dust (top), or as foil-wrapped pills (center). Some users inhale the powder; others sprinkle it on cigarettes or marijuana joints (bottom), which they smoke.

rock concerts, we can also chart the changing fashions of drug use in the youth culture as a whole,"[11] they wrote in the study.

Newmeyer and Johnson, both sociologists, worked on the "Rock Medicine" staff of the Free Clinic during the 1970s, where they helped provide first aid to members of rock concert audiences in the San Francisco area. The two Free Clinic staff members found that when people were brought into concert first-aid stations in violent and combative states, they had probably taken PCP. From 1973 to 1977, Newmeyer and Johnson said, the Rock Medicine first-aid stations treated 36 patients under the influence of phencyclidine. "Of the 36 cases, four were noted as having been particularly violent during treatment; other symptoms commonly mentioned were 'rigid,' 'disoriented,' 'stumbling,' 'hyperactive,' 'unresponsive,' and 'incoherent,'" they wrote. "More than half of the PCP victims had used the drug in combination with alcohol, which frequently contributed to the nature of the problem."[12]

Cheap and Available

PCP grew in popularity because it is cheap, available in a variety of forms, and can be manufactured quickly and simply with chemicals that are easy to obtain. Today, the price for a single hit of PCP can be as low as five dollars. One of the reasons for the low price is that phencyclidine can be cooked in a homemade lab—all that is needed is a bucket or steel drum, some glass tubing, a source of heat, and the chemicals. A batch of the drug, with a street value worth thousands or even millions of dollars, can be created in less than a day.

Depending on the skills and resources of the drug makers, phencyclidine can be made into a powder, which is inhaled through the nose, or sprinkled on marijuana so it can be smoked. Also, it can be produced in pill or liquid form and ingested. Typically, the user will soak a marijuana cigarette in liquid PCP before lighting up. Tobacco cigarettes can be used if marijuana is not available. Sometimes, to give PCP an extra kick, the drug maker will add formaldehyde or potassium cyanide to the recipe. Formaldehyde is a component of embalming fluid; potassium cyanide is employed to kill insects, among other uses. With formaldehyde or potassium cyanide in the mix, it should come as no surprise that most PCP users admit the drug does not taste very good.

During the 1970s, the powder form of phencyclidine was quite common, and drug users took to calling it Angel Dust. The drug has been known by dozens of other street names, though, includ-

PCP's Price on the Street

Phencyclidine is like most commodities that are available for sale in the American marketplace. For these products, including PCP, pricing depends on where the item is sold, how much is available, and how great the demand is. For example, in today's market a small bag of powdered PCP can be bought on the streets of Philadelphia for as little as $5, while an ounce of liquid PCP, which is enough to lace several cigarettes or marijuana joints, can cost as much as $350. In Washington, D.C., a single cigarette dipped in PCP, which is known as a wet, can be bought on the street for $25, while in Cleveland the street price for a wet is $10. Clearly, prices fluctuate from city to city and also depend on the form of the drug.

Since PCP dropped out of sight for a period during the 1990s, the DEA believed it unnecessary to track the drug's street price during that time. The agency resumed tracking PCP's price in 2000. In 2004, the DEA estimated that a gallon of liquid PCP could be sold for as much as $20,000 in New York City. While most drug dealers who operate underground labs sell PCP by the ounce rather than the gallon, some do sell it in large quantities to other street dealers, who then peddle the drug in the smaller quantities.

The DEA reports that the street price of a liquid ounce of phencyclidine in New York City is $400. Comparing this price to the price for a gallon of liquid PCP clearly shows the substantial profit potential in the PCP business. At $400 an ounce, a single gallon of PCP can bring in over $50,000 on the New York streets—or more than twice the $20,000 that the lab charged the street dealer for the gallon. In short, the street dealer can reap a profit of more than $30,000.

Certainly, there is evidence that PCP profits can be enormous. In 2003, police raided a home in Baltimore and found thirty gallons of liquid PCP as well as more than two hundred gallons of raw chemicals needed for the manufacture of the drug. Police estimated that the street value of the contents of the lab could have been more than $50 million.

ing Hog, Ozone, Rocket Fuel, Wack, Crystal, Love Boat, Tic, and Embalming Fluid. Marijuana cigarettes laced with PCP have been called Killer Joints, Super Grass, Fry, Lovelies, Wets, Waters, and Dippers.

Regardless of which names are used for PCP, there has never been another drug like it on the street. When somebody is on a PCP high, there is no telling what he or she will do. When taking low doses, PCP users report dreamy, euphoric experiences. The problem is, though, that most PCP users find that they are not satisfied to remain on low doses. They crave PCP and must take larger and more frequent doses. When that happens, there can be violent, dangerous, and tragic results. PCP users often lash out at friends, family members, or strangers for no reason at all. By the early 1980s, newspapers would often carry stories reporting terrible and senseless acts of violence committed by people under the influence of phencyclidine. In the Washington, D.C., area, phencyclidine was known as the "Keys to St. E's" because PCP users picked up by police were often thought to be mentally ill and so were taken to St. Elizabeth's psychiatric hospital for evaluation. "It's a painkiller," said Vincent Thomy, a St. Elizabeth's clinical psychologist. "That allows people to smash glass from windows and rip moldings around doors because they feel nothing."[13]

One twenty-four-year-old PCP user described his violent actions while on the drug to researchers Jennifer James and Elena Andresen:

> When I get violent on PCP the main theme seems to have something to do with biting people on their necks. I've been known on at least six occasions to have attacked people. They didn't know that I was approaching them—to attack them actually. What I would do was to walk up to them, grab them by the shoulders, I guess, and bite them in the neck, or attempt to bite them in the neck, and wrestle with them actually—no hitting or striking motion. If I can get to their neck, I sink my teeth into the skin. On one occasion me and a friend of mine were using PCP. We had injected a massive dose of PCP. When I came to I was in the drunk tank of a local jail, and my friend's jaw area was completely swollen and we had burn marks on our hands, and it looked as though we had placed our hands on a hot burner. . . . We never did find out why we both had burn marks on our hands, how they got there, or how his jaw got broken.[14]

Another trend that became obvious to emergency room physicians was that many PCP users did not know they were taking it. The hapless phencyclidine victims bought the drug thinking that it was LSD or cocaine or, in later years, Ecstasy. Another PCP user described her first time to James and Andresen:

> I didn't know that's what it was. It was powder and we had put it on a joint and smoked it. The guy at school was selling it, and so my girlfriend and I and her boyfriend and that guy, we smoked a joint. He called it angel dust. I didn't know what it was. He had it in tinfoil, and he was just selling it. I didn't think that it was anything really bad because of the name. I just thought it had something to do with weed or something because he had sprinkled it on like a cigarette smoke and said it just was really, really strong and just smoke it through.[15]

Stories of unsuspecting PCP users continue to crop up today. Recently, a Connecticut teenager named Mike told a *Newsweek* reporter that when he smoked his first marijuana cigarette, he had no idea it was laced with phencyclidine. Because he was not a veteran pot smoker, Mike did not realize the pungent taste of the drug meant something else had been added to it. Instead of the dreamy, feel-good marijuana high he had been told by his friends to expect, Mike felt paranoid and prone to violence. "The next day, when most people would feel normal, I would still have trouble walking. I felt like I wanted to hurt people," Mike said. "I felt like everybody was after me."[16]

PCP Refuses To Go Away

Abuse of PCP continued on an upward trend during the early 1980s. DAWN reported that hospitals treated 4,983 PCP emergencies in 1982 and 6,123 in 1983—a rise of more than 20 percent in a single year. PCP-related deaths jumped as well, from 156 in 1982 to 217 in 1983. But just as it seemed phencyclidine use was taking off, consumption of PCP took a sudden and dramatic turn downward. Emergency room visits by PCP users declined, and so did the number of overdose deaths. Had phencyclidine users finally realized the drug was too dangerous and unpredictable? Probably not. Drug agencies attributed the decline in

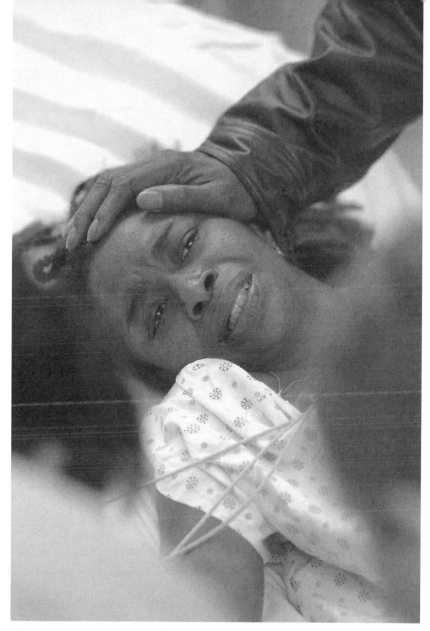

Hospital workers face a challenge when caring for people under the influence of PCP, because these patients are often violent and hard to restrain.

PCP use to the growing availability of crack cocaine and the so-called club drugs, such as Ecstasy and Rohypnol. People were simply switching drugs. During the late 1980s and the first half of the 1990s, phencyclidine use declined. In 1990, the *Monitoring the Future* survey reported that just 1.2 percent of high school

Dramatizing PCP Abuse

Hollywood has created many movies that portray life in the drug culture. Over the years, films such as *Reefer Madness*, *The Trip*, *Panic in Needle Park*, and *Easy Rider* have examined heroin, marijuana, and LSD use. The abuse of phencyclidine, although explored to a lesser degree than these other drugs, also has been shown on movie screens as well as on television. In most of these dramatizations, PCP users are depicted as either evil characters or innocent victims who suffer tragic consequences.

In the early 1980s, television programs like *Quincy* and *The White Shadow* featured shows that focused on PCP use. In the 1982 film *Death Wish 2*, Charles Bronson played a timid architect named Paul Kersey who is driven to vigilantism after his daughter is kidnapped and raped by gang members. Kersey tracks down the rapists, one of whom had evaded prison by convincing authorities that he was insane and under the influence of PCP when he committed the crime.

Early in her career, actress Helen Hunt played a PCP-using teenager in two made-for-television movies. Hunt (who would go on to star in the hit television comedy series *Mad About You* and win an Academy Award for her role in the 1997 film *As Good As It Gets*), portrayed these drug-abusing characters in *Desperate Lives*, an hour-long ABC After School Special that aired in 1982, and in the feature-length *Angel Dusted*. In *Angel Dusted*, which aired in 1981, Hunt's character, Lizzie Eaton, consumes PCP, then commits suicide by throwing herself out of a second-story window.

More recently, in the 2001 film *Training Day*, Academy Award–winner Denzel Washington played a corrupt cop named Alonzo Harris, who tricks his new partner into smoking a PCP-laced marijuana cigarette.

seniors had experimented with PCP—an all-time low. By the mid-1990s, PCP use was believed to be so rare that the DEA stopped tracking the street price of the drug.

Still, phencyclidine use did not stay on a steady decline for long. During the second half of the 1990s, use of the drug started increasing again. Between 1998 and 2002, DAWN reported a more than 100 percent increase in emergency room visits by PCP users. In 2002, DAWN said, 7,648 patients on PCP were treated in hospital emergency rooms, a vast increase over the 3,436 cases reported in 1998. What is more, in 2000, the National Household

Survey on Drug Abuse, which is conducted by the U.S. Substance Abuse and Mental Health Services Administration (SAMHSA), reported that 264,000 Americans were believed to be using phencyclidine. Not surprisingly, all these higher statistics for PCP were being recorded while DAWN was also reporting that use of Ecstasy and similar club drugs appeared to be leveling off. Evidently, people were switching back to PCP. "We now find an apparent resurgence in emergency department episodes involving PCP,"[17] a DAWN report concluded in 2002.

Criminals Target Young People

The increase in phencyclidine use may have much to do with the criminals producing the drug. In the 1970s and 1980s, PCP was usually manufactured by an individual cooking a batch of the drug in a basement lab. Once the drug was produced, he would sell "hits" to a steady and regular clientele. Now, however, the PCP trade has been taken over by notorious street gangs who oversee extensive networks capable of manufacturing millions of dollars worth of the drug.

Particularly troubling to drug experts is that these criminals have targeted young people as PCP customers. In 2003 police in Fairfax County, Virginia, confiscated a batch of phencyclidine pills stamped with the image of a Pokemon character. In another case in 2004, Chicago police confiscated lollipops laced with PCP. The lollipops were fashioned in the shapes of maple leaves, pumpkins,

Police officers have discovered lollipops like this one laced with PCP.

and Santa Claus heads, and came in bright shades of green, yellow, and red. They sold on Chicago streets for ten dollars each, according to police. "We put out the community alert to notify parents and children," Chicago Police spokesman Sergeant Edward Alonzo told a news reporter. "We don't want kids to be using [the lollipops.]"[18] During one recent period in Houston, emergency room doctors at Ben Taub Hospital found themselves treating as many as five PCP users a day, most of them between seventeen and twenty-five years old. And in Washington, D.C., during 2003, Inspector Hilton Burton, the head of the city police Major Narcotics Branch, said children as young as twelve were found to be using PCP.

Although the majority of the new PCP users are believed to be poor blacks and Hispanics from the inner cities, there is no question that teenagers from middle-class suburban homes are also experimenting with phencyclidine. Police in rural Lancaster County, Pennsylvania, have made PCP-related arrests. So have police in the towns of Stamford and Greenwich, Connecticut—two of the wealthiest communities in the United States. "Wet started being used in the inner city, but it is hitting the suburbs,"[19] Cynthia Hepler, an admissions manager at a Houston drug treatment center, told a reporter.

Certainly when Drs. Victor Maddox and Graham Chen were attempting to find a new anesthetic they had no inkling that their work would eventually unleash one of the most unpredictable, addictive, and deadly drugs on the American public. Whether PCP users experimented with the drug in the 1970s or discovered PCP after its reemergence in the 1990s, whether they live in tough inner-city neighborhoods or comfortable suburbs, people who use phencyclidine share one common characteristic: they risk incurring long-lasting, and possibly even permanent, effects on their brains and their bodies.

 **Chapter 2**

The Physical Effects of PCP

Even a small dose of phencyclidine can cause dramatic changes in a user's behavior. The PCP user can suddenly erupt into an uncontrollable rage that may last for hours or even days. Long-term users find they have to take more and more of the drug to achieve the high they seek. In the meantime, their brains and bodies are undergoing permanent changes. While experiencing their highs, PCP users lose touch with reality. They may injure themselves or suffer fatal accidents because, unaware of their surroundings, they have walked out of windows or drowned in their own bathtubs. Other PCP users suffer depression and other symptoms of mental illnesses that have led them to commit suicide. There is no question that PCP users put themselves at risk the first time they ingest the drug.

Small Dose Just Not Enough

PCP begins affecting the user within minutes of being taken, causing him or her to experience many strange feelings. Even a small dose of phencyclidine, typically no more than three to five milligrams, can cause effects that last for five or six hours. PCP may cause a person to feel dizzy, as though he or she has consumed too much alcohol. The user may feel somewhat numb and achy. He or she may break out in a sweat, or feel flushed as blood pressure increases and pulse quickens. The user may also experience frequent urges to urinate.

Psychologically, many first-time PCP users have reported the drug creates a cloudy haze of euphoria. One user told researchers about his experience while under the influence of a small dose. "Immediately after smoking the Dust (PCP) I started experiencing the effects," he said. "All my troubles seemed to go away. I felt a little drunk and had some trouble walking around the apartment. Objects appeared either very far away or very close and I couldn't really judge distance at all. . . . [I] felt outside my body for most of the trip."[20]

Like most drug abusers, people who take PCP are rarely satisfied with small doses. Although PCP is not known to create a physical addiction, which is the case with drugs like heroin and nicotine, the phencyclidine user nevertheless craves larger and larger doses, believing that the modest and pleasant feeling of euphoria experienced on the smaller dose will be intensified if he or she takes a larger hit. The user could not be more wrong. When the PCP user steps up to a larger dose of ten milligrams or so, the feelings of numbness will intensify. The user will feel uncoordinated and prone to stumbling. His or her mind will race in a hundred different directions. One college student describes his experience under the influence of a ten-milligram dose of PCP: "I feel like I can't think . . . And I can't express myself even if I can think because it's hard for me to talk. My lips are numb. It's so uncomfortable. My perception is very bad. Nothing is clear . . . My mind is just a complete blank . . . I have such a strange feeling. I can't explain it. Like I'm still asleep, yet I'm not asleep."[21] In these cases, it could take as long as forty-eight hours for the PCP user to shake off the effects of the trip.

Many PCP users constantly seek to increase their dosage, believing that the next high is sure to be better than the last. When the user starts ingesting PCP in amounts that exceed ten milligrams, however, he or she is likely to experience the full and terrible consequences of the drug. The PCP user will experience an increased rate of breathing. High doses may cause nausea, vomiting, blurred vision, flickering of the eyes, drooling, loss of balance, and dizziness. Speech may become slurred or garbled. Blood pressure, pulse, and respiration drop to very low rates. The PCP user may collapse into a coma.

While the physical effects that result from PCP use may vary, it is the drug's impact on the brain that causes a user to exhibit bizarre behavior. PCP's dissociative qualities cause the user to experience hallucinations. One PCP user named Don described his

A sense of death, or "out-of-body experience," is a common hallucination among PCP users.

hallucinations to researchers Jennifer James and Elena Andresen, who studied phencyclidine abuse in the cities of Seattle and Tacoma, Washington:

> [After] two to five seconds the mind-altering effects of the drug become apparent and I would enter the state of PCP disorientation, the state where disassociation was the norm. My stimuli was scrambled. I would perceive something in . . . a way that would allow me to look at it in almost what I would call a clear, total clarity. I would be able to look at a situation as well as an object without its social values, or cultural values. But that wouldn't necessarily give me the freedom then or even the urge to destroy the object or cast it aside, or that person. . . . Instead it would put me in kind of a contemplative attitude. . . . It does seem to have some kind of property that . . . allows me to get a distance between myself and the world, and for a time, dissociate myself from the world. There's a lot of body noise, and a lot of mind noise that goes along with the use of this drug in these effects that I'm talking about, but that noise is secondary to this feeling of detachment and it has to be put up with.[22]

Later, Don told James and Andresen, "The time sense that PCP gives me, the way it affects my time sense, it stretches it out, it negates it actually and puts me in the 'eternal now' which for me is infinity. The past never was and the future never will be. All that exists is me and the here and now, with countless billions of possible ways I might go at any given moment."[23]

PCP users generally feel emboldened, fearless, and reckless. Their senses deceive them: they see images that are not there, hear phantom sounds, smell aromas that do not exist. They exhibit delusional behavior and suffer from symptoms that mimic schizophrenia and paranoia. They can turn violent, particularly in response to the false realities they experience. Indeed, the newspapers regularly report grisly stories of violent, uncontrolled behavior by PCP users. Researchers who studied PCP use in women asked participants to describe their experiences under the influence of the drug. Typical comments included, "I would fight anyone who touched me," "When high, I would attack people. I was extremely violent," and "My head would tell me things that were not true or were not there. It seems someone was always after me."[24]

The effects of a high dose of PCP may not wear off for several days. Phencyclidine is easily stored in body fat, which means the

The PCP Trip

Many chronic phencyclidine users have no recollection of what happens to them while they are under the influence of the drug. Others who have taken mild doses have reported hallucinating and, more specifically, seeing themselves and objects assume strange shapes and unusual proportions. These users suffer from "microscopia" and "macroscopia"—conditions in which the concept of size is scrambled.

A PCP user can gaze at a small object, such as a baseball, and seemingly see it growing in gigantic spurts until it is the size of a building. Or the user may think he sees his or her own arm stretching for hundreds of feet. Or the user may look in a mirror and imagine seeing his or her own head shrink to the size of a pea. "A common theme is 'astro-traveling' while high—imaginary trips through outer space," wrote drug abuse researchers Jennifer James and Elena Andresen in *Angel Dust: An Ethnographic Study of PCP Users*. "The 'Alice in Wonderland' trip is also common—part of the body gets very big or very small."

Another common condition that PCP brings about is temporary "antegrade amnesia," which causes the user to lose the memory of events that may have occurred just seconds before. Indeed, a person under the influence of PCP often is unable to tell whether an event has just happened, is currently happening, or is about to happen.

These conditions as well as others have prompted the National Highway Traffic Safety Administration to label PCP a drug that should never be used in any quantity by anyone who plans to drive. In a study of fifty-six drivers who were arrested and found to be under the influence of PCP, the agency determined that all of them were impaired and unable to safely negotiate the road. In its "Drugs and Human Performance Fact Sheet," the agency warns, "The use of PCP is not compatible with skills required for safe driving. Severe impairment of mental and physical abilities can occur following single doses."

drug can stay in the user's system for a long time. In fact, PCP has shown up in urine tests more than a month after use. A former phencyclidine user named Jackie told a reporter about the drug's long-term effects on her. "I thought I could control it, but I found myself moving to another level with it," she said. "I started hallucinating, I started seeing bright lights and images. I thought about committing suicide. Some nights, I'd get high in my apartment and just start hollering and screaming. A couple of

The drug causes people to feel bold and indestructible, but also paranoid and delusional. These feelings often combine to make PCP users violent.

times, I just started taking my clothes off. I just felt really hot, and I had to get out of my clothes. I'd sit in a tub of cold water for hours until the trip would just go away. Then I realized, you know, 'This is just crazy.'"[25]

Delivering Too Many Messages

When someone ingests phencyclidine, he or she is introducing a drug to his or her brain that will block or stimulate neurotransmitters—the chemicals that carry messages from one brain cell to another.

Each person has millions of brain cells, known as neurons. Each neuron emits electrical impulses containing messages that control the body's functions. These impulses travel along large stems known as axons and smaller stems known as dendrites. When an impulse reaches the end of an axon, it jumps over a tiny space, known as a synapse, on its journey to the dendrite of the next neuron. As the electrical signal makes the jump, the brain cell releases a neurotransmitter chemical to carry the message. Accepting the message on the end of the dendrite is a group of molecules known as receptors. These receptors can only accept specific neurotransmitters. This is how the neurons of the brain work together to tell a foot to take a step, a hand to hold a pencil, or lips to form words so that a person may speak. Not all neurotransmitters carry messages, however. Some neurotransmitters block unwanted messages from jumping from cell to cell.

Drugs affect the natural transmission of information in the brain. A drug may overstimulate the neurotransmitters, so that too many messages are delivered to the neurons. Or, it may neutralize the neurotransmitters that work to block unwanted information, causing a flood of unwanted messages to reach the neurons. Still another possibility is that the drug may act as its own neurotransmitter, sending its own messages to the brain cells.

Drugs such as nicotine, cocaine, and marijuana prompt the brain to release a neurotransmitter called dopamine, which enables the body to move and also regulates emotions, particularly the feeling of pleasure. Constant use of those drugs over time will permanently affect the brain's usual operations. Specifically, when too much dopamine is released, the brain compensates by reducing the number of dopamine receptors. Also, because the brain is responding to the stimulation of the drug to create dopamine, the body may make less dopamine on its own. These changes in the brain means that a drug user may find it hard to feel happy during the periods when he or she is not under the influence of drugs. Like these other drugs, phencyclidine is also known to affect the transmission of dopamine. A sudden surge in dopamine absorbed by the brain would explain a PCP user's mood swings, as well as the user's stumbling and lack of coordination.

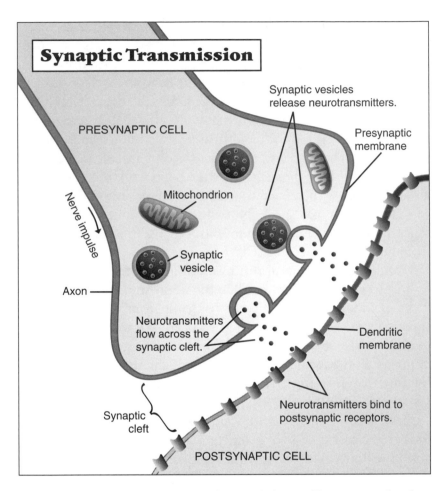

In addition to dopamine, phencyclidine affects several other neurotransmitters. For example, PCP affects the transmission of serotonin, a neurotransmitter that controls sleep, sensory experiences, and mood. Scientists believe that people on PCP hallucinate because the drug boosts the level of serotonin in their brains. Another neurotransmitter affected by PCP is glutamate, which controls a person's learning ability, excitability, and perceptions of pain. PCP enhances the transmission of glutamate, which explains why the phencyclidine user is often in an excited state and hard to calm down. This also explains why a person under the influence of PCP does not feel pain when he or she is injured.

Because the drug desensitizes users to pain, they can sustain severe injuries because they simply are not aware that they have hurt themselves by crashing through a window or trying to punch through a wall.

PCP and Schizophrenia

Phencyclidine subjects its users to terrible physical and psychological consequences, but in recent years medical researchers have found a positive use for the drug. More specifically, since phencyclidine causes the same symptoms in its users as the symptoms often suffered by people with the mental illness schizophrenia—namely hallucinations, delusional behavior, and a distorted sense of reality—scientists have used the drug to explore the roots of schizophrenia.

One study concentrated on the flow of the neurotransmitter glutamate in the brain. Lab rats were injected with PCP, which soon caused them to run frantically around their cages or constantly swivel their heads—symptoms believed to parallel schizophrenic behavior in humans. Researchers discovered that the PCP had pumped up the release of glutamate in the rats' brains, prompting these scientists to hypothesize that if they found a drug that could safely block glutamate, it could be used to help control symptoms of schizophrenia in humans.

Another study concentrated on the neurotransmitter dopamine. In this study, monkeys were injected with PCP. Soon, the monkeys exhibited bizarre behavior, such as repeatedly trying to grab a banana that was out of reach. It was found that phencyclidine reduced the amount of dopamine produced in the monkeys' brains, leading scientists to speculate that a drug that would increase the flow of dopamine might be effective in treating schizophrenia.

Scientists are encouraged by the results of these studies and are convinced more research is needed. Writing in the May 2002 issue of *Journal of Psychology*, psychologist John B. Murray explained that "schizophrenia is so complex a disorder that no one factor can account for all its symptoms." He warned, though, that researchers would do well to proceed with caution if they hope to use PCP to learn the truth about the causes of schizophrenia. "Many questions must be answered before this dangerous drug can be safely studied as a means of uncovering the action of PCP on schizophrenia symptoms and a new approach to treatment," Murray wrote. "Which actions of PCP are involved in behavioral effects of PCP in humans? Is PCP addictive? Do subjects develop tolerance to it? PCP may open a new look into schizophrenic symptoms, but many questions about its effects remain unanswered."

A PCP user's immunity to pain poses a special challenge to the police officer who encounters the user. Gary Hankins, an official of the Washington, D.C., Fraternal Order of Police, told a reporter, "A lot of the self-defense techniques that our officers use rely on pain. You hit someone in the shin with a night club, you hit them on the elbow or forearm, that pain will subdue them. The people on PCP that we see are often impervious to the pain. Sometimes, an officer will just have to wail away on someone like that because he sees his own life in jeopardy trying to control this person."[26]

Finally, PCP also affects the neurotransmitter norepinephrine, which controls blood pressure and pulse rate. This explains why the PCP user may find his or her blood pressure and heartbeat skyrocketing or dropping to dangerously low levels while under the influence of the drug.

Long-Term Effects

The long-term physical effects of phencyclidine use can be substantial. The user may experience memory loss, speech difficulties, weight loss, reduced blood pressure, respiratory problems, and kidney failure. These problems may continue for years before the patient improves. Additionally, a young person who uses PCP may not grow properly or develop intellectually because his or her hormones may be affected. PCP users experience depression and other serious psychiatric effects as well. Long-time PCP users report that they sometimes experience flashbacks—hallucinations that occur even when they are no longer using the drug. These flashbacks can occur weeks, months, and even years after they used the drug.

Drug abuse researcher Harvey W. Feldman writes:

> Of all the adverse effects that were possible, the one that concerned PCP users the most was 'burning out.' It was abundantly clear to all the users that sustained and regular use of PCP would lead inevitably to burning out, a condition that was described as appearing 'spacey.' In this condition, a user was usually incoherent, unable to think clearly, forgetful with severe memory loss. As a result of these symptoms, the user generally developed a reputation as unreliable and lacking in fun and spontaneity, all characteristics that run counter to those features adolescents tend to value. [27]

PCP causes serious long-term effects, including depression, physical ailments, and memory loss.

Even those who use PCP say they are concerned about "burning out." Burnouts "just talk like they don't know what they're talkin' about, they don't care," a PCP user named Linda told drug abuse researcher W. Wayne Weibel. "You know, they talk like 2-year-olds, you know, you give em a hard question, it'll take em about . . . half hour to figure it out. . . . But, I think tic [PCP] burns ya out more than anything else. If people like start talkin' to me and I notice I'm not even listening to em, you know? I'm in another world, you know? I'm getting burnt out. Or if I didn't do any tic and I still feel high, you know? You gotta still have some in your system, you gotta be kinda burnt out. You know?"[28]

Pregnant women who take PCP—even if only occasionally—place their babies at risk. The drug passes through the placenta to affect the unborn fetus. As a result, a child born to a PCP-using mother may be mentally retarded or physically deformed.

When PCP is laced with toxic substances, the user faces another set of health issues. For example, some users dip marijuana cigarettes into liquid PCP laced with formaldehyde, to produce a "wet" joint. When formaldehyde is heated above three hundred degrees, which occurs when a wet is lit with a match, the chemical breaks down into carbon monoxide—a highly toxic gas. Aside from being exposed to this gas, the user of the wet marijuana cigarette experiences other side effects, including a disorganization of thought and decreased attention span. Over a long period of time, smoking PCP treated with formaldehyde can cause bronchitis; destruction of body tissue; impaired coordination; lung damage; and sores in the nose, throat, and esophagus. One very serious effect of smoking PCP laced with formaldehyde is that the toxic chemicals will destroy brain cells.

An Endless Circle

The health problems caused by PCP abuse are complicated by the fact that the drug is addictive. It leads to cravings and compulsive behavior by users seeking their next dose. Certainly, one long-term effect of PCP use is the lifestyle of addiction led by the chronic user. The person who becomes addicted to phencyclidine lives his or her life devoted to finding more of the drug.

A typical chronic user was Kathy, a Washington, D.C., resident who spoke with a news reporter about her life as a PCP addict. Kathy said her exposure to PCP started in college. "I had a friend who cooked PCP," Kathy told the reporter. "We used to be able to get it pure. I remember we once got a small garbage can full of [liquid] PCP up to the dorm. The crowd of people I was hanging with was pretty heavily into it. It wasn't like I felt I had to challenge this drug. There wasn't any talk of the dangers. I just always wanted something that would keep me up and alert and moving."[29]

Soon, the PCP took its toll on Kathy's studies. Because the drug affected Kathy's short-term memory, she found it difficult to remember what she had just read. When her grades started falling, Kathy reduced her PCP use and managed to graduate.

Still, Kathy found it hard to completely eliminate her PCP habit, and soon after graduating she found herself once again addicted to the drug. For months, she used PCP constantly, spending thousands of dollars on marijuana laced with phencyclidine. Her life was a cycle of getting high, coming down, going to work, and getting high again. Kathy was fired from many jobs because

Deadly Combinations

Taking too much PCP can be fatal. An overdose of the drug can cause respiratory arrest, which is the inability to breathe. An overdose of phencyclidine can also cause heart failure and a dramatic increase in body temperature. Indeed, it is not unusual for PCP users to find their body temperatures rising to more than 105° Fahrenheit (40° Celsius), which can lead to kidney failure and brain hemorrhaging. Studies have shown that a twenty-milligram hit of PCP can cause users to slip into a coma.

However, it is nearly impossible for users to know how much is too much, because the drug is manufactured in unregulated underground labs, making the actual potency of a dose anybody's guess. Another factor is that, as with many drugs, over time PCP users build up a tolerance to the drug. Therefore, it will take heavier and heavier doses for chronic users to achieve the high they seek.

Further adding to the risk of overdose is the PCP users' habit of mixing the drug with alcohol or other drugs. SAMHSA reports that in 2001, 74 percent of all PCP users admitted to hospitals had either alcohol or another drug, usually marijuana, in their systems. Some of the harder drugs that users typically take with PCP are cocaine, crack, and LSD, all of which can create deadly combinations. Statistics show that five of six people who die from overdosing on phencyclidine ingest a second drug shortly before their deaths.

Paramedics prepare to treat a man who has overdosed on drugs. The potency of PCP varies from dose to dose, so it is impossible for users to know how much will be fatal.

Serious accidents are common among PCP users because of the dissociation from reality caused by the drug.

her PCP use made her an unreliable employee. Her personal life also changed drastically for the worse because of her drug addiction. "I think I did things I never would have done otherwise when I was heavily into PCP," she said. "I remember I broke into this guy's house because I knew he had just gotten a fresh batch [of PCP] in. I waited for him to leave and then called on the phone to make sure no one was home, and then I broke in. I had sex with people I didn't want to have sex with just to get PCP. It got to the point where I didn't want to have anybody over because I wanted it all for myself."[30]

A family member came to Kathy's rescue. Her mother forced her into a drug-treatment facility. She spent fifteen months in drug treatment, but after leaving the program Kathy soon fell back into her old ways. In fact, to celebrate her "graduation" from drug treatment, Kathy smoked marijuana laced with PCP. "I thought I could just get high on the weekends or whatever. But it really doesn't work that way," she said. "It takes you down a little further the second time, because you know what you're doing is not right. I was ashamed. There were people [at drug treatment] who looked up to me. I'd come back and visit them, and they'd know I was back on [PCP], and they'd be real nice and say, 'When are you coming back?' It took me a while to put my ego in my pocket and come back in for help."[31]

Kathy eventually reentered drug treatment. Her second journey through the program was more successful than her first. Yet even after completing the second treatment course, she focused on living drug-free one day at a time, always aware that she could fall back into the endless circle of PCP addiction.

Never Coming Down

While Kathy's case illustrates that it is possible to end a PCP habit and live a productive life, there are nevertheless many people who hope to never come completely down from their PCP highs. When not under the influence of the drug, many chronic PCP users report severe depression and other mental anguishes and, therefore, they prefer to be high all the time. What they fail to realize, however, is that when they are under the influence of phencyclidine they are in a state that is dangerous to themselves and others.

One researcher found: "Chronic users clearly enjoy PCP and experience it in a positive way . . . Most say it takes a few days to return to normal, but many of them don't bother to and use the drug every day . . . [they] almost always complain of being spaced and worry about turning into 'vegetables.' They are noticeably depressed when not high, so much so that some have committed suicide at this point. Serious accidents are commonplace among users. Almost all report having been in an automobile accident or knowing someone who was, while on PCP. Falls are common, even off cliffs or out of boats and windows. Impairment of motor and sensory functions makes many normal physical activities dangerous."[32]

Cases of PCP overdose are common and can result in death. Many PCP users, afflicted with depression during the times when they are not high, have turned to suicide. It is very common, though, for PCP users to fall victim to fatal accidents because they have dissociated from reality—they think they can fly, so they step out of a window, for example. "A large number of deaths have occurred in association with phencyclidine intoxication," wrote the authors of a study on young PCP users. "In the majority of cases the immediate cause of death was . . . drowning, or trauma."[33]

In fact, the study found, the most common reason for a PCP user's death was not the drug itself but the bodily injuries the user sustained while under the drug's influence. According to the study, "The user could not indicate where his limbs were in rela-

Cough Medicine That Acts Like PCP

Many pharmacies have found they have to restrict the sales of non-prescription cough medicines to teenagers because the medicines contain dextromethorphan, or DXM, which many users believe can give them a PCP-like high. (While in small doses and when used as directed medicines containing DXM can be effective cough suppressants, in large doses, DXM can cause hallucinations.) Between 2000 and 2003, the number of DXM overdoses reported to poison control centers in America more than doubled, rising from 1,623 in 2000 to 3,271 in 2003. It is believed that some 120 non-prescription products, most selling for less than ten dollars, contain DXM.

For many young people, the problem with trying to get high on DXM is that a large quantity is needed to achieve a hallucinogenic effect. If teenagers ingest such a large quantity, however, they can get sick, because cough medicines typically contain other ingredients that cause illness when taken in excess. Still, teenagers persist in abusing cough medicines. In Cleveland, one boy drank an eight-ounce bottle of cough syrup, consuming some seven hundred milligrams of DXM. Later, he told John Horton of the *Cleveland Plain Dealer* newspaper, "I remember pleading for my life, to just get through it . . . I felt like when my eyes were closed I was getting bigger and was about to burst out of the walls of my room. My skin literally felt like it was on fire, and I couldn't stand the pain anymore."

Deaths from DXM overdoses are rare, but they still occur. Pam Jones's fifteen-year-old daughter Samantha died after consuming nine non-prescription cough tablets that contained DXM. Now Ms. Jones visits high schools near her home in Ohio, giving talks to students on the dangers of DXM abuse. She always shows the students a photograph of Samantha's gravesite. Jones told the *Plain Dealer*, "I tell them, 'This is where Samantha spent her 16th birthday. That's the price she paid.'"

tion to three dimensional space or could not respond appropriately to imminent danger . . . 'Street' doses of phencyclidine may seriously interfere with the user's ability to swim, drive, climb at heights, flee from a fire or sense imminent danger."[34] In some cases, PCP users have frozen to death because they ventured out on winter nights dressed inappropriately, never feeling the freezing temperature and its effect on their bodies. One heavy drug user related to researchers Jennifer James and Elena Andresen how he sustained a severe injury while under the influence of PCP:

> One time I was in a tavern and smoking right there in a booth in the tavern quite openly and I blacked out, and my roommate at the time was smoking with me also. He was a person who is very aware of the effects of the drugs, specifically the effects of the drug on me. He got me out to his car just so I wouldn't be flailing about in public and then when I got inside the car, inside that contained space, I started flailing about and in the process of trying to subdue me I fractured one of his ribs; and at that point he had it with me and quit trying to restrain me and let me go back into the tavern. And upon entering the tavern I approached a woman at the bar and started to proposition her in apparently a gross, vulgar manner, and her boyfriend, who was a total stranger to me, tried to persuade me not to make the advances to his young woman. Whereupon I proceeded to grab his sweater and pulled it over his head. Well, he hit me right between the eyes and knocked me flat on my back; and whether it was from the punch or the PCP or both, I was knocked out until I came around a few hours later. And I don't know if I was coming out of the effects of the dust or the knock on the head. It was quite a severe blow, and I still bear the scars today.[35]

The above story illustrates that a PCP user engages in behavior that is foreign to his or her usual personality. While the user experiences greater difficulties as he or she increases his intake of the drug, the user often does not realize the serious long-term effects the drug use has on his or her body. However, the people who use PCP are not the drug's only victims. Many other people are impacted by PCP abuse. It impinges not only on innocent bystanders but primarily on friends and family members of PCP users, as well as the police officers who have to make arrests, the social workers and medical professionals who try to rehabilitate the users, and all citizens who must shoulder the burden that PCP use places on society.

 **Chapter 3**

The Effect of PCP on Society

Phencyclidine affects not only the drug user but also that person's friends and family members, because often they are the ones who must find a way to help the user overcome his or her addiction. The drug also puts a strain on society: The police and courts must respond to PCP users; innocent citizens find themselves victims of crimes committed by people high on PCP; and governments and human services agencies must devote money and staff to drug treatment programs. Even the environment is affected by PCP, because the dangerous chemicals used in the manufacture of the drug are often recklessly dumped into rivers or even right onto streets.

Trouble for Society

Regardless of whether people live in big cities, suburbs, or small towns, they are often affected by PCP use. For example, in June 2004 police in tiny Beacon, New York, found a seventeen-year-old female stumbling through the streets, screaming in panic. They summoned paramedics, who took the young woman to the hospital. "She said her heart was racing and her throat felt like it was burning," Police Sgt. Louis Musmeci told the *Poughkeepsie*

Journal. "She thought she was dying."[36] Once the teenager arrived at the hospital, doctors quickly concluded that she was under the influence of PCP.

Only a month later, Beacon police had another encounter with a PCP user when they found a car parked across a street, blocking traffic. When they asked the driver to step out of the vehicle, they found a dazed and disoriented New York City man who thought he was in a train station. He repeatedly asked the police officers for directions. When the officers placed the man in the back seat of a patrol car, he turned violent and tried to kick the

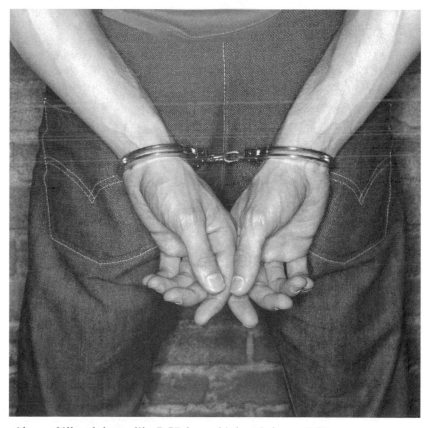

Abuse of illegal drugs like PCP has a high social cost. PCP users present a danger to themselves, to others around them, and to the police who are charged with getting them off the streets.

windows out of the car. Later, medical tests confirmed what Beacon police suspected—that the man was under the influence of phencyclidine.

Another dangerous PCP-fueled situation occurred during 2002 in the small community of Quakertown, Pennsylvania, when nine-

The Diminished-Capacity Defense

When Sikia Smith went on trial in Nevada for the murders of four men, his attorney admitted to the jurors that there was little doubt his client had played a role in the crime. Smith stood trial in 1999 as one of three men charged with the murders. However, Smith's attorney, Tony Sgro, invoked the so-called diminished-capacity defense, arguing that Smith was mildly retarded, suffered from attention-deficit disorder, and had used PCP the night of the slayings. "This case is about an individual who is a foolish follower," Sgro told the jurors, according to the *Las Vegas Review-Journal*.

People who plead diminished capacity hope to convince jurors that although they may not be insane, they are still not responsible for their crimes because they did not comprehend the severity of their actions at the time the crime was committed. The reason they often cite for their failure to tell right from wrong is the influence of drugs, particularly PCP. "Since PCP intoxication can resemble closely some forms of schizophrenia, superficially it would appear to be an ideal candidate for defenses of diminished capacity," explains Ronald K. Siegel, psychiatry professor at the University of California at Los Angeles. "PCP intoxication can show all the essential ingredients for such a defense: altered consciousness wherein the defendant's attention, awareness, and ability to respond meaningfully to the environment and situation are disturbed; mental confusion regarding the meaning of the act or its consequences; involuntary behavior which might prevent optional courses of action; and interference with goal-directed behavior so as to prevent organizing and directing physical movements."

Even so, diminished-capacity defenses are rarely successful, at least when invoked to win a not-guilty verdict. Therefore, instead of following that strategy, a defense attorney usually will argue diminished capacity in the hopes that the jury will find the defendant guilty of a lesser degree of the crime. In Smith's case, he was convicted of first-degree murder, but the jury sentenced him to life imprisonment. Clearly, the evidence of his diminished capacity had a bearing on his sentence. Another of Smith's codefendants, who did not invoke a diminished-capacity defense, received the death penalty.

teen-year-old Joshua David Herder threatened two priests in a Roman Catholic church with a knife. Local police took Herder into custody, and he was taken for psychiatric observation at a local hospital. The next day, he broke out of the psychiatric ward and stole an ambulance that was idling in front of the hospital. Police followed the ambulance back to the church, where they arrested Herder. Authorities later determined that Herder had been under the influence of PCP during this episode. The drug made Joshua "paranoid and fearful," Herder's attorney told the judge who heard the case. "It also made him feel like Superman—like he could do anything."[87]

A National Problem

PCP abuse occurs in small communities all over the country, not just on the East Coast. For example, in Lufkin, Texas, police found a man wandering the streets with his pants down. When police approached him, the man would not respond to their questions. Finally, the man fell down and could not stand up again by himself. Later, he admitted to police that he had been smoking phencyclidine.

Considering the type of bizarre behavior phencyclidine is known to trigger, the police in Beacon, Quakertown, and Lufkin should feel fortunate those cases ended without serious injury to themselves, innocent people, or the PCP users they took into custody. Yet other communities have not been so fortunate. In September 2003, twenty-four-year-old Reginald Dwayne Mayes took PCP in combination with other drugs and went out for a drive. Soon he was heading the wrong way down a busy Houston highway. Mayes' car crashed head-on with another vehicle, which was carrying four adults and five children. Six people died in the crash, including Mayes, two of the adults in the other car, and three of the children. Sergeant T. L. Herndon of the sheriff's department in Harris County, Texas, told a reporter for the *Houston Chronicle*, "PCP is just a nasty drug. It causes hallucinations, very cyclical behavior— being calm one minute and very crazy and out of your mind the next minute. PCP by itself would put a person in a condition where they can't function, let alone drive. It would be hard enough to walk down the street to make it to a destination."[38]

Another PCP user caused a violent tragedy in New York City. In this case, thirty-year-old Larme Price started using PCP after the September 11, 2001, terrorist attacks. Under the influence of the drug, Price found himself consumed by paranoia and went on a killing spree, believing he would rid the city of terrorists. During February and March of 2003, Price murdered four immigrants, all shop owners in the city's working-class neighborhoods. "One man's twisted view led to the murders of four innocent people,"[39] Vito Spano, commander of the police task force that tracked down Price, told the *New York Daily News*. Price pleaded guilty and was sentenced to life in prison.

Similarly disturbing is the case of rapper Antron "Big Lurch" Singleton, who was arrested in Los Angeles after police found him standing in the street, naked and covered in blood. When police investigated, they found that Singleton had murdered his twenty-one-year-old girlfriend. She had bite marks on her face, a slashed cheek, and a lung that appeared to have been gnawed on. Singleton admitted to smoking PCP the morning of the murder. In 2003, he was sentenced to life imprisonment.

Even more bizarre is the case of Marc Sappington, a twenty-five-year-old Kansas City man convicted of killing three friends, including a teenager whose body was dismembered and partially eaten by Sappington. When he confessed to police, Sappington said that when he was under the influence of PCP, voices in his head told him to commit the murders and eat the flesh of his victims. When Judge J. Dexter Burdette sentenced Sappington to life in prison, he told the defendant, "You are the closest thing to a homicide time-bomb there is. There is no way I am going to endanger the community again."[40]

No Typical User

If PCP use occurs in communities as diverse as Beacon, Lufkin, Quakertown, New York City, Los Angeles, Houston, and Kansas City, then clearly it is a widespread national problem. The truth is

While under the influence of PCP, users may commit crimes that they would never consider while sober.

that there is no typical PCP user: addiction to the drug cuts across racial, age, and gender lines.

A study by SAMHSA on PCP users looked at the demographic makeup of patients admitted to drug treatment facilities. In 2001, the report stated, some 8,200 phencyclidine users were admitted to drug rehabilitation centers in the United States. The report noted that 49 percent of the patients were black while 26 percent were Hispanic. In addition, 19 percent of the patients were white, while the remaining 6 percent were composed of patients of other races.

Meanwhile, there is evidence that suggests use of the drug is growing among female users as well as African-Americans. A report by DAWN that charted emergency room visits by phencyclidine users noted a 63 percent increase in female patients from 2001 to 2002, when 2,738 women were treated for overdoses and similar PCP emergencies. The number of black patients increased by 28 percent during that same period. In 2002, the report said, 3,308

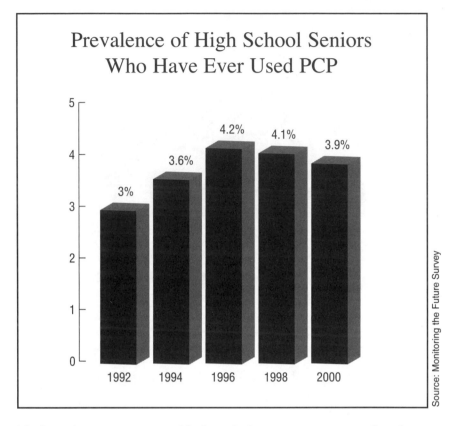

Prevalence of High School Seniors Who Have Ever Used PCP

Source: Monitoring the Future Survey

black patients were treated in hospital emergency rooms for phencyclidine overdoses and similar problems.

"Those who are today using PCP tend to come from a different place, both socio-economically and in their drug-taking behavior," concluded researcher Arthur Stickgold in the late 1970s. "PCP is, today, becoming the drug of choice of the lower class oppressed minority group member seeking an escape from persecution. In the past, s/he has found this escape in other depressant drugs such as heroin and barbiturates."[41]

Nearly ten years later, Vincent Thomy, the St. Elizabeth's psychologist, also noted that lower-income and disenfranchised people [those deprived of a privilege or legal right] often use PCP. He told a reporter, "I think a lot of drug taking in general has to do with feeling powerless. It's interesting, though; I've noticed this power perception on PCP more with men than women. It varies, but in general with women I noticed more the dissociative, dreamy, floaty type of escape. With men it was more power."[42]

Costly to All

Regardless of who uses the drug or where the user may live, the individual who takes PCP distresses his or her friends, family members, and, certainly, the taxpayers. Government leaders in Bucks County, Pennsylvania, learned that fact through unfortunate circumstances when an inmate in their county prison fell into a coma after ingesting PCP he had smuggled into his cell. Since the inmate was in the county's care, the county was responsible for his medical expenses. The inmate spent some six months in a hospital recovering from the coma, running up medical bills that totaled more than $300,000. The county government had no choice but to pay the bills.

While $300,000 is a lot of money, that sum represents only a very small slice of the tremendous costs that illegal drug use inflicts on society. According to the DEA, Americans spend some

---

PCP's Youngest Victims

Perhaps the most unfortunate victims of PCP abuse are the children born to mothers who use the drug before or during pregnancy. These women's addictions often cause their babies to suffer from birth defects and other problems that affect their physical and mental development.

A study conducted at the University of California at Los Angeles in 1990 found that infants whose mothers used PCP weighed about a pound less at birth than normal infants. They were also, on average, about three-quarters of an inch shorter from head to heel than babies whose mothers were not exposed to phencyclidine. Additionally, the circumferences of these babies' heads were an average of approximately a third of an inch less than those of normal babies.

Furthermore, the study showed that young children whose mothers used phencyclidine were slower learners than normal children, and they suffered from several developmental disabilities. For example, the PCP-affected children exhibited jitters, tremors, irritability, weaker muscles, and slower reflexes.

Drugs, guns, and money seized in a raid are displayed in a police station. Federal agencies estimate that the sale and abuse of illegal drugs like PCP cost American society billions of dollars each year.

$65 billion per year on illegal drugs, while use of PCP and other drugs annually costs the American economy $98.5 billion in lost earnings, $12.9 billion in health care costs, and $32.1 billion in other costs, including social welfare costs and the cost of goods and services lost to crime.

It is difficult to break those numbers down and assign specific costs to specific drugs, but there are some indications of the contributions PCP makes to the drug addiction problem in America. In particular, the DEA has performed a city-by-city analysis of drug use among people who have been arrested. In that analysis, for example, the agency reports that 8 percent of all males arrested in Cleveland and 4 percent of all females arrested in that city tested positive for PCP, which were the highest rates in the country. Other cities where a significant number of arrestees tested positive for PCP were Oklahoma City, Seattle, Philadelphia, Houston, and Dallas. Meanwhile, SAMHSA reports that 47 percent of all PCP users who enter rehabilitation are directed there by the criminal justice system. Essentially, then, nearly half of all known PCP users end up in police custody.

Pain for Friends and Family

Friends and family members of PCP users are often affected by the drug in some way. Some may succumb to pressure from their drug-abusing friend and try PCP themselves. That was the case with a young man named Michael, who started smoking PCP at age seventeen. Five years later, Michael found himself in prison on murder and robbery charges. He blames peer pressure in high school for getting him hooked on PCP. "All the kids were smoking it in high school, particularly girls," Michael told a reporter. "They really love this drug."[43]

Michael's story is far from unique. In Anne Arundel County, Maryland, eighteen-year-old Ervin Montague was sentenced to thirty years in prison for the murder of Aaron Howard, thirty-three, whom Montague said was as close to him as a "big brother or an uncle"[44] would be. Montague told police he smoked PCP before the murder and that Howard had supplied him with the drug. Although prosecutors said they found no evidence to suggest that Howard gave the drug to the teenager, an autopsy did find evidence of PCP in the victim's body.

Perhaps the best-known case of PCP abuse involving two people with a very close relationship is the tragic story of singer James Brown and his third wife, Adrienne. Born into poverty in rural South Carolina, Brown became a gospel singer in the 1950s, then switched to singing rhythm-and-blues music. By the 1960s, Brown found himself propelled to the top of the R&B charts as the renowned "Godfather of Soul." James and Adrienne met in the early 1980s, when he made a guest appearance on the television music program *Solid Gold*. At the time, Adrienne worked as a hair stylist for artists who appeared on the program, and by 1984 she and Brown were married.

It soon became clear to many people who knew the couple that they had serious substance abuse problems. In 1988, Brown was charged with striking his wife with an iron pipe and shooting a gun at her—charges that were eventually dropped when Adrienne refused to testify against her husband. Next, he started missing concerts. Then, in May 1988, Brown walked into an office building he owned in Augusta, Georgia, where an insurance company was holding a seminar for salesmen. Bursting into the seminar, Brown brandished a gun and threatened members of the audience.

A police chase through parts of Georgia and South Carolina ensued, ending when the singer crashed and his pickup truck flipped over. When police caught up with Brown, they found him singing to himself and dancing by the wreck. "He was obviously under the influence of something, and it wasn't alcohol,"[45] said Sgt. Frank Tiller of the Richmond County, Georgia, sheriff's department. Brown was found to be under the influence of PCP. But even months after the crash, the singer refused to acknowledge he had a drug problem. "What's PCP?"[46] he asked, when a reporter questioned him about his drug use. Eventually, Brown was sentenced to six years in prison, although he was paroled after serving two years.

Continuing Drug Problems

The same year that James Brown was arrested, Adrienne Brown also faced PCP-related charges stemming from a number of incidents. In one case, she was charged with setting a small fire in a New Hampshire hotel room. In another, she was arrested at the Augusta, Georgia, airport with two vials of liquid PCP hidden in her blouse.

By the time James Brown was released from prison, the couple still had not overcome their drug habits. In early 1996, Adrienne Brown died shortly after undergoing routine cosmetic surgery. The coroner ruled that Adrienne suffered from heart disease and obesity stemming from chronic drug abuse. The autopsy showed that she had consumed PCP shortly before the surgery and that the drug evidently reacted badly with the prescription painkillers the doctors gave her following the operation. According to an official with the Los Angeles County Coroner's Office, the cause of death was ruled "PCP intake and . . . heart disease."[47]

Following the death of his wife, James Brown continued to struggle because of his drug problem. In 1998 he was hospital-

Singer James Brown and his wife Adrienne refused to admit their drug problems. Adrienne Brown's death in 1996 was related to her PCP abuse.

ized for an addiction to prescription painkillers; he fought his habit, eventually resumed his singing career, and remains a beloved figure to his fans. During his struggle against drugs, Brown told a Georgia judge hearing his case, "My life has always been a model, and I just don't feel good about it now . . . If I had it all to do over again, well, I just wouldn't do it . . . I hope this is behind us."[48]

Environmental Catastrophes

In addition to the individual human tragedies of PCP, the manufacture of PCP has an impact on the environment that sets its production apart from that of other illegal substances. The making of PCP requires chemicals typically used in industrial applications. Most of those chemicals are highly toxic and flammable.

While chemicals used to make PCP are legal and useful when they are employed for their intended purposes, those same chemicals are hazardous to people and the environment if used and dis-

A variety of toxic chemicals are used to illegally manufacture PCP, and they are often disposed of improperly. Dumping of these chemicals can cause great harm to the environment.

posed of improperly. Among the chemicals used to make PCP are bromobenzene, which is a solvent that is also employed as an additive for motor fuels; cyclohexanone, a solvent used as a polisher and degreaser, meaning it is useful in stripping oil and grease from metal; phenylmagnesium bromide, which is explosive when it comes into contact with water; piperdine, which is used as an ingredient in fuels and is often employed to help rubber harden; and potassium cyanide, which serves as an insecticide, among its other uses.

Companies that use those chemicals for legitimate purposes must follow strict regulations established by the U.S. Environmental Protection Agency to dispose of the substances. But illegal PCP labs follow no precautions when they dispose of their waste chemicals. In one 2003 case, when the DEA announced the arrests of thirteen men in a Los Angeles-based PCP ring, the agency found their lab could have caused a significant environmental catastrophe. The DEA explained in a statement:

> Some of the chemicals used include ether, which is highly flammable and explosive, sodium cyanide, and a lethal poison. Exposure to sodium or potassium cyanide could be acutely toxic or deadly if cyanide gas is present. Phenyl magnesium bromide [PMB] is also commonly used during the manufacturing of PCP. PMB reacts violently when introduced to water. PCP manufacturers often store large quantities of these dangerous chemicals in residential neighborhoods without regard to the safety and welfare of their neighbors. Individuals manufacturing PCP have dumped the residue associated with their narcotics manufacturing in locations which are frequented by unknowing citizens. Innocent people exposed to these chemical dumps could possibly be seriously injured due to inhalation of the chemical fumes.[49]

In 1995, a resident of Charlotte County, Virginia, told local officials that somebody was dumping trash off a bridge into Ward's Creek. When officials investigated, they discovered the trash contained the waste sludge left over from the illegal manufacture of PCP. Their investigation led them to the arrests of two individuals, whom they charged with not only making the illegal drug but with dumping the waste chemicals into the environment. In the case, a California man received a prison sentence of forty-eight years, for producing at least four million doses of the drug, and an additional five years, for "felony hazardous waste violations"[50] stemming from the illegal transportation and dumping of the waste into the environment. A second individual was sentenced to five years in prison on conspiracy charges.

Clearly, PCP affects more than just the drug user. Family, friends, and many others with whom the user comes into contact —sometimes merely innocent bystanders—suffer as well. Additionally, the drug burdens the criminal justice system, social services agencies, and even environmental protection agencies. There is no question, though, that the primary victims of phencyclidine are the users themselves, who must be convinced to give up their habits or face the possible consequences of jail, damaged lives, and even death. Many users do successfully free themselves from their habits, but most of them find that doing so requires a long and difficult trek that often takes years to complete.

 **Chapter 4**

Coming Down from the High

Phencyclidine users who truly seek to rid themselves of their addictions face a lengthy, arduous struggle. Rehabilitation can take months or even years. In many cases, recovery includes many hazardous turns and frequent setbacks, since few PCP users are able to give up their addictions without occasionally returning to the drug.

First Step: The Hospital
Often, recovery starts at the local hospital, where the PCP user must be physically restrained and isolated until the narcotic effect of the drug wears off. A recent case that occurred in Texas provides a good example of this. After Houston police were summoned to arrest a disoriented woman covered in blood and wandering the streets, officers found the woman carrying a broken shard of glass, which she had used to terrorize a family and, evidently, slash her own wrist. It took several officers to subdue the twenty-nine-year-old woman. Finally, an ambulance arrived. The woman was restrained and placed in the ambulance, which then headed for the city's Ben Taub Hospital.

Violent PCP users who are brought to a hospital's emergency room are typically injected with tranquilizing drugs. This helps prevent injury to the patient or the medical staff.

The drama was not over, however. As the ambulance arrived at the hospital's emergency room, the woman broke free from her restraints and fought with members of the ambulance crew. Again, police had to step in and subdue the woman, who continued to resist as she was trundled into the emergency room. The woman was reported to have been under the influence of a drug, most likely PCP.

These events illustrate that any time a PCP user goes to the hospital, whether on his or her own or in the custody of police, the user may still be in a wild and uncontrollable state. Indeed, emergency services workers must take many precautions and follow special procedures in an attempt to gently ease the PCP user down from his or her high. And yet, despite all the precautions, easing the user down is not always possible.

Many hospitals have developed specific procedures for treating the phencyclidine user. Typically, once the PCP user is in the emergency room, physicians will inject the patient with tranquilizing drugs to calm him or her down. Doctors usually will not release the patient for at least twelve hours, to ensure normal vital signs and a subdued mental state.

Hospitals often isolate the user in a sealed room, adjacent to the emergency room, that is stripped of furniture as well as electric appliances, such as televisions and medical equipment, which make noise or generate bright light. Nurses and doctors are advised to not even talk to the PCP user, since the patient may be easily incited. In the room, the PCP user is restrained in the bed—although not necessarily through the use of straps, since the user may injure himself by fighting against them. Instead of using straps, many hospitals advise their medical staffs to roll the PCP user tightly in a bed sheet, as though they are swaddling a baby. Yet regardless of how they choose to restrain the user, medical professionals know that curbing the individual's movements is vital because of the violent nature of someone under the influence of PCP. "When people say they've been using fry [the street term

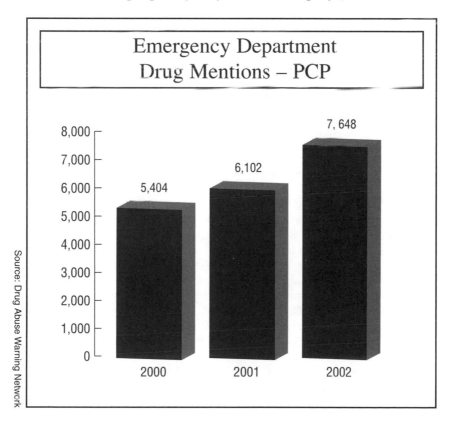

Emergency Department Drug Mentions – PCP

Source: Drug Abuse Warning Network

for a marijuana cigarette dipped in PCP] and they come into the emergency room and are just wild—they have to be strapped down in their beds or they destroy the room—that tells me that PCP's in there,"[51] said Jane Maxwell, a spokesperson for the National Institute on Drug Abuse.

When the user is calm, doctors will flush the PCP from the patient's system, usually through an intravenous drip. Patients coherent enough to help with their own recovery are urged to drink cranberry juice, which acts as a diuretic, meaning it will cause urination. However, if the user has taken such a large dose of phencyclidine that his or her life is in danger, the doctor may order the patient's stomach pumped.

After recovery in the emergency room, PCP users are occasionally admitted to the hospital for observation. Phencyclidine can cause a high fever as well as erratic breathing and irregular heartbeats that continue after the narcotic effect of the drug has worn off. PCP can also cause a malady known as rhabdomyolysis, which is a breakdown of muscle fiber. Rhabdomyolysis is a serious illness because the loose muscle fiber accumulates in the kidneys, where it can cause damage and perhaps become life-threatening.

A PCP user admitted to the hospital will likely undergo a psychiatric examination to determine whether the drug has con-

The Milk Myth

Some people who use PCP believe that all it takes to come down quickly and easily from the high is a tall glass of milk. When using PCP, they are careful to keep a carton of milk nearby, believing that if the trip proves to be unpleasant, all they need to do is drink the milk to recover. Sharon Weidenfeld, a Virginia-based private detective who has investigated many PCP-related cases, told *Insight on the News* magazine, "When people smoke dippers, they are often unable to move. The common belief is that the user has only to drink some milk to become unstuck. A conscientious PCP smoker simply makes sure to have some milk on hand in case of an emergency." In reality, however, the belief that milk can cure the bad PCP trip is purely a myth, according to Weidenfeld. Milk actually has no effect at all on PCP, she said.

What Happens in a Drug Test

The U.S. Supreme Court has ruled that schools can require students participating in "competitive" extracurricular activities, such as sports, to take drug tests. In the working world, many employers now require job applicants to pass drug tests before they are hired. Once hired, the testing is not necessarily over for employees; for example, many of those who work in security-sensitive jobs—usually as police officers or prison guards—are subjected to random testing, meaning their employers can require them at any time to submit to a drug test.

For a drug test, usually urine is analyzed in a process known as gas chromatography-mass spectrometry, or GC-MS. In this process, a sample of urine is treated with a gas that causes it to break down into its components and stick to a gel coating on the inside of the testing chamber. Next the components are fed through a strong magnetic field that enables the mass spectrometer to record their molecular weights. Then the results of the test are checked against a database of molecular weights assigned to different drugs, including phencyclidine.

How effective is the test? The GC-MS test is believed to be highly accurate and capable of detecting very small traces of the drug. In the case of phencyclidine, the GC-MS test can detect as little as twenty-five nanograms of PCP per milliliter of urine. A nanogram is .000000001 of a gram. Additionally, not only can minute traces of the drug be found by the GC-MS test, but, because PCP is retained in fat cells, the drug can be found in urine weeks after being ingested.

tributed to a mental illness. At the St. Elizabeth's psychiatric hospital in Washington, D.C., PCP users have been forced to remain in a bare, cell-like special-treatment room (STR) for fifteen days while they come down from their highs and are evaluated for mental illness. The room features just a single window, covered with wire mesh; a staff member looks in on the patient every fifteen minutes. "PCP users are easily excited by any stimulation, even simple things such as light, noise, and touch," explains Dr. Matt Weissman, a clinical psychologist at St. Elizabeth's. "The STRs offer a sort of sensory-deprivation therapy that has proved not only effective but popular among PCP patients. PCP patients respond very well to the special-treatment rooms. Some of those who have been in a hospital before even ask to go into one of the rooms, because they know they'll feel better."[52]

Finally, when the PCP user's vital signs stabilize, doctors will urge him or her to enter a drug treatment program. If police brought the PCP user to the emergency room, after the user comes down from the high he or she will probably enter the criminal justice system. In this case, a judge may order the user to enter a treatment program.

Long and Difficult Struggle

A patient who is dedicated to rehabilitating himself or herself will undergo a long and difficult struggle. PCP addictions are among the hardest to break because the user faces some unique challenges. For example, a PCP user often has no memories of his or her experiences while under the influence of the drug. For some addicts, bad experiences that occur while under the influence of drugs or alcohol can be a key motivator to quit, but because the PCP user generally cannot remember what he or she did, bad experiences provide little motivation to stop abusing the drug.

Another challenge involves the method of giving up PCP. A person who wants to quit a drug like heroin, which causes a physical addiction, can substitute a medication called methadone that helps suppress the addict's cravings. However, there is no medication that can be administered to a PCP patient to wean him slowly from addiction. The PCP user has no choice but to give up the drug entirely—to go "cold turkey."

Rehabilitation has other components as well. Typically, experts in detoxification work with the PCP user to change his or her lifestyle, diet, attitudes, and commitments to employment and family. Counseling is a big part of PCP detoxification; a user is taught how to make good decisions, face problems, and lead a drug-free life. Counselors work with the PCP user both individually and during group sessions, in which the user is encouraged to talk about his or her addictions and peers help each other through crises.

The ability of the PCP user to give up the drug largely depends, of course, on the user's resolve and willpower. Studies suggest that the chronic PCP user who commits himself or herself to overcoming the habit suffers many setbacks before achieving total

Counseling sessions, during which users learn how to overcome their dependence on PCP, are an important element of drug treatment.

detoxification. According to SAMSHA, the typical PCP user first seeks detoxification at the age of eighteen, yet the average PCP user in a rehabilitation program is twenty-eight years old. In other words, the norm for those addicted to PCP may be an on-again, off-again rehabilitation period of more than ten years.

A study published in the *American Journal of Drug and Alcohol Abuse* provides information on why rehabilitation is so difficult for the PCP user. The study focused on PCP users undergoing detoxification at a Los Angeles rehabilitation center. It reported that the main hurdle faced by counselors was convincing PCP users that the drug was bad for them. "All our subjects expressed 'psychological dependence' on PCP, as manifested by liking the drug and great difficulty in stopping its use despite serious adverse consequences,"[53] wrote the study's author. The study also indicated that drug counselors may have to work for months or even years to overcome a user's belief that PCP provides an outlet from his or her troubles that he cannot find elsewhere. As study author David Gorelick reported:

> There was frequent group consensus on the psychological effects of PCP and motivations for its use. The two main psychological effects often cited

as maintaining PCP use were the feelings of strength, power, and invulnerability it engendered; and a psychic numbing that was used to self-medicate dysphoric affects, especially anger and rage ("I use PCP because I want to forget"). Some subjects were attracted by the challenge of the risk in using PCP, i.e., not knowing what would happen. Three types of acute intoxication responses were described: stimulation, depression, and hallucinogenic. . . . Almost all subjects had had religious experiences while intoxicated: feelings of meeting God, impending death, etc.[54]

Other researchers have also found that PCP use often prompts the user to believe he is either near death or already dead. According to drug addiction researcher Harvey W. Feldman:

One of the more consistent hallucinations that PCP apparently triggered—and this same phenomenon occurred in even the early studies when PCP was being experimented with as a legitimate anesthetic—was a sense of death, called in the scientific literature *meditatio mortis*. Users often reported this strange byproduct of the high. Although their reactions were often fearful and triggered periods of crying, they often found the experience exciting and enticing. In a kind of out-of-body experience that made them something like Tom Sawyer viewing his own funeral, users reported a pleasant sensation associated with feeling like the "living dead."[55]

Gorelick wrote that the thirty-seven PCP users who participated in his Los Angeles study remained in the treatment program an av-

Symptoms of PCP Withdrawal

Heroin users develop a physical addiction to the heroin drug. To kick their habits, they must overcome severe and painful withdrawal symptoms that include profuse sweating, muscle and bone pain, cold flashes, abdominal cramps, diarrhea, vomiting, and muscle spasms. Unlike heroin addicts, however, PCP users generally do not become physically addicted to the drug, but the chronic phencyclidine users still must endure withdrawal symptoms when they decide to end their drug habit.

PCP withdrawal symptoms are psychological—the user must fight a mental craving to use the drug. For example, when resisting the drug, PCP users may find themselves battling depression, laziness, and an increased need for sleep. To help fight the craving for the drug, some users eat large amounts of food. Such symptoms usually last for at least a week, but can continue for several weeks, depending on the user's history of addiction as well as his or her resolve to stay drug-free.

erage of twenty-one weeks, although some stayed for as little as one week, while others participated for as long as one hundred and fifty-five weeks. While in treatment, nearly 80 percent of the users provided "hot" urine samples to drug counselors, meaning PCP was detected in their urine while they were undergoing rehabilitation. Obviously, most of the PCP users continued to use the drug to some degree even while they were undergoing rehabilitation. After following the users in and out of treatment for a year, the researchers reported that just four of the PCP users had remained drug free for the entire twelve months. The others either continued in the program, dropped out of treatment, sought a residential treatment program in which their detoxification efforts would be stepped up, or wound up in jail. "Our experience with outpatient treatment of PCP abuse was only marginally successful . . . Our results are consistent with previous comments on the difficulties of treating PCP abusers,"[56] concluded the study's author.

Acting out Common

A similar study followed a group of adolescent PCP users who were committed to a residential drug treatment program, meaning they lived away from home in a facility dedicated entirely to their detoxification. Juvenile authorities believed that these young people could not be trusted to remain off drugs by living at home and visiting a rehabilitation center a few days a week; they believed that these users needed twenty-four-hour attention from drug counselors who watched their every move. The study concentrated on how the young people responded to the counseling sessions and other treatment techniques employed at the residential center.

For starters, the study found that the best therapy for the young PCP users was for them to attend school. Therefore, as part of the treatment center's program, the facility's educational staff provided classes as well as tutoring in routine school subjects. Even though the educational staff did not set high goals for the students—good grades were not considered important, for example—the researchers felt that the young people benefited from an educational environment, particularly the young PCP users who continued to manifest physical and mental symptoms from the drug, such as memory loss and sluggish or uncoordinated movements. "Individual attention provided by the educational tutors, coupled with the educational testing and the learning diagnostician's work, give the client a sense that he/she will soon be able to function normally,"[57] said the study's authors.

Still, the researchers found that rehabilitation of young PCP users was no easy task. Acting out by the clients was common and, in fact, expected behavior. Staff members tolerated hostile and angry behavior, responding by trying to avoid confrontation with the young people and isolating them in safe, nonthreatening environments. The young clients were expected to have little interest in the counseling sessions. The researchers reported:

> They are usually unable to cope with the demands and expectations of a structured, intensive therapy regimen. With these clients, staff expectations are drastically lower. This means that the PCP abuser is not expected to participate extensively in either group or individual therapy, school or recreation programs. It is understood that he/she may be belligerent and refractory [unresponsive] to treatment. Hostility, agitation, and depression, as well as memory loss and motor impairment are considered part of the pathology to be treated. . . . Certain acting out behavior is tolerated in these clients, more so than in clients having no history of PCP abuse. Generally, acting out behavior takes the form of extreme verbal abuse. We assume that these outbursts of anger and hostility will occur and we work with them, rather than prohibit the behavior and thereby exacerbate the situation.[58]

The study also centered on the clients' length of stay in the drug treatment center. The average length of stay at the center for young people who used drugs other than PCP was fifty-six days. For adolescents who admitted to occasional use of PCP, the average length of stay was reported at seventy-three days. And chronic PCP users found themselves spending an average of seventy-nine days at the drug treatment center. Clearly, the study confirmed what many addiction experts have been saying about phencyclidine for years: when it comes to drug habits, addiction to PCP is among the toughest to break.

Recovering drug addicts share a room in a residential treatment center in New York. Studies indicate that detoxification is most successful when accomplished in centers such as this one.

Wiping out the Urge

Still, recent developments in medical science may hold some hope for PCP users in rehabilitation. Researchers at the University of Arkansas have developed an antibody from the tobacco plant that, when injected in lab rats, appears to block the narcotic effect of PCP for as long as two months. No doubt, there may be years of research ahead before the antibody is ready for humans; nevertheless, if the procedure proves to be successful, it will mean that a PCP user can visit a doctor every few weeks and receive an injection that will help him fight the urge to ingest phencyclidine. "If someone enters into a treatment plan, you might give them a dose of this antibody so that if they slipped during the program and tried to use the drug, they would not get the rewarding effects of it and they may continue with the therapy," said Michael Owens, a University of Arkansas pharmacology and toxicology professor. "We're hoping to get them through the weak moment, through that difficult period of trying to kick their habit."[59] An additional benefit of using the tobacco plant antibodies is that they work instantly, the Arkansas researchers found, so a PCP user's urge can be virtually eliminated within seconds.

Antibodies are present in all human blood, where they serve as disease fighters. An antibody attaches itself to a virus and then gives a signal to a healthy cell to eat the invading bug. The tobacco plant antibodies help block the effects of PCP by attaching themselves to the phencyclidine molecules, making them too big to move from neuron to neuron. With no room to maneuver, the PCP heads for the liver, where it is filtered out of the body without the user feeling the narcotic effect of the drug.

The tobacco plant antibodies have also been found to be effective in killing the urge to use methamphetamine, a stimulant that causes its users to exhibit frantic behavior. The Arkansas scientists injected lab rats with PCP or methamphetamine, then watched them scurry around their cages, each traveling as much as one-half mile a day. That behavior mimicked the excited pace of human users of PCP and methamphetamine. But after injecting the rats with the antibodies, the researchers watched the rats slow down significantly. "In four minutes, it's sitting in a corner cleaning itself, starting to get a little bored. In other words, the therapy works,"[60] explained Ralph Henry, a University of Arkansas biology professor.

While the research appears to be promising, relief for the PCP user through medical science is still very much in the future. In the meantime, the user looking to end his or her addiction must be determined and ready to handle setbacks that are likely to occur during the lengthy and difficult process. At the same time, the battle against PCP use will continue to be fought in the hospitals and rehabilitation centers as well as on the streets, where law enforcement agencies target illegal labs as well as the notorious gangs of dealers who have taken over what has proven to be a lucrative underground business.

 **Chapter 5**

The War on PCP

O ver the past several decades, the United States has conducted a vigorous war against drugs, including PCP. Lawmakers have enacted stiff penalties on narcotics dealers in an effort to keep dangerous drugs off the streets. Meanwhile, police carry on a city-by-city, neighborhood-by-neighborhood fight against PCP, in an effort to shut down the clandestine laboratories that produce the drug. Police officers must be inventive as gangs employ new, sophisticated methods to avoid detection. The difficulty of fighting the war on drugs is not made easier by the fact that there is no national strategy to combat PCP use.

A Constant Struggle

As with most drug-prevention efforts, the war against PCP is constant. Law enforcement agencies must continually be on the lookout for dealers, illegal labs, and distribution networks. Work by undercover officers and tips from community sources help police target those who peddle drugs on the streets. But arresting these low-level dealers does not have much impact on the illegal distribution of PCP, because as soon as they are locked up others take their places. To stop the flow of drugs, the police must identify and arrest drug kingpins. Finding those directing the drug trade, and establishing a solid case against them, often involves difficult investigations that can take months to complete.

Efforts by law enforcement agencies sometimes result in significant drug busts. For example, in the summer of 1997 sixteen members of a violent Los Angeles street gang known as the Bounty Hunters were arrested on charges of making and distributing some $30 million worth of PCP. When authorities announced the arrests, they believed they had broken up a ring controlling most of the PCP sales in Southern California. "It is a significant [case] in that we believe this . . . organization controls the PCP sold in L.A. County or at least most of L.A. County,"[61] said Los Angeles County Deputy District Attorney Maria Ramirez.

An undercover police officer detains a suspected drug dealer during a raid. Since the mid-1980s, the U.S. government has aggressively conducted a "war on drugs."

The case of the Bounty Hunters illustrates how much work is involved in making such a high-profile bust. To begin with, the police got a lucky break when a citizen noticed a gang member dumping waste chemicals into an alley and notified authorities. Once the police knew where the gang members were dumping the chemicals, they were able to set up a surveillance system and secretly follow the drug dealers as they visited the labs, met with customers, and delivered their goods.

Highly Organized and Hard to Stop

The Bounty Hunters case also shows the high degree of organization in street gangs that produce and sell drugs. The agents who investigated the Bounty Hunters alleged that in the three years they had followed the activities of the gang, its illegal labs produced no less than one million doses of PCP. In addition to purchasing thousands of dollars worth of raw chemicals and cooking the PCP, gang members were alleged to have worked out a distribution system that included leasing trucks and hiring a network of dealers who peddled the drug on Los Angeles streets.

And the Bounty Hunter arrests also show an important problem law-enforcement officials face in the war on drugs. Despite breaking up the Bounty Hunters' drug ring, the bust did not put a permanent dent in the PCP trade. Instead, once the Bounty Hunters were taken off the streets, members of other gangs quickly filled the void. Soon, according to the U.S. Drug Enforcement Agency (DEA), PCP was just as easy to purchase in Southern California as it had been before authorities broke up the Bounty Hunters' drug ring.

According to the DEA, during the past decade PCP distribution in many cities has been taken over by street gangs who are amassing millions of dollars in illegal profits. "These organizations operating mainly in Los Angeles, and, to a lesser extent, in Houston, supply most of the PCP available in the nation," states a 2003 DEA report. "The recent emergence of large PCP laboratories in other locations, such as Indiana and Maryland, are cause for concern because this may be an indication that PCP is on the rise."[62]

Prevention through Penalty

As with any illegal drug, making and selling PCP is a risky proposition, and the people who traffic in the drug face severe consequences if they are caught. In 1978, the federal government declared PCP a Schedule II drug, making it illegal to manufacture and distribute phencyclidine. By then, PCP's potential as a commercially available horse tranquilizer had even been abandoned. Categorizing phencyclidine as a Schedule II narcotic meant drug dealers could face stiff penalties for selling PCP—from five years in jail for the first offense to as much as life imprisonment for repeat offenders. And depending on how much PCP was sold, there could be mandatory minimum sentences imposed as well.

In 1986, Congress passed the U.S. Anti-Drug Abuse Act, which mandated prison sentences for drug dealers caught selling certain quantities of drugs—even if it is their first offense. In the case of PCP, a drug dealer convicted of selling at least ten grams faces a mandatory minimum sentence of five years in prison without parole, while a dealer caught selling one hundred grams faces at least ten years in prison without parole.

Congress adopted the harsher mandatory minimum sentencing for drug dealers after the tragic death of University of Maryland basketball star Len Bias. Bias had been drafted in 1986 by the Boston Celtics of the National Basketball Association. To celebrate, Bias took cocaine. He died of a drug overdose.

One of the most powerful lawmakers in Congress at the time was Democrat Thomas P. "Tip" O'Neill, the speaker of the U.S. House of Representatives. O'Neill represented a Boston district in Congress. His constituents were outraged by Bias's death, and they demanded that Congress get tough on drugs. In response, O'Neill pushed for the tough Anti-Drug Abuse Act. Both Republican and Democrats supported the measure, which President Ronald Reagan signed into law in the fall of 1986.

Over the years, advocates for prison inmates have argued that the law discriminates against first-time offenders; they contend that the penalties are much too harsh. These critics point out that a first-time offender who sells a few hundred dollars worth of

Crips and Bloods

Authorities believe Los Angeles County is home to some 1,300 gangs. While the region's estimated 150,000 gang members include Hispanic, Asian, and white youths, the vast majority are black. These African Americans belong to gangs affiliated with either the Crips gang or the Bloods gang. Many of them deal drugs, including phencyclidine.

The Crips were started in 1969 by fifteen-year-old Raymond Washington. Washington had been turned down for membership in the Black Panther Party because he was too young, yet despite the rejection, he remained inspired by the party's goals of black power and revolution. As a result, he started his own group with the aim of making it a political force of young black people. Yet instead of building political clout, those who joined the new group soon fell into crime. Since many of them took to carrying fancy walking canes, they were nicknamed the Cripples, which was soon shortened to the Crips. Some gang members adopted the term "crippin'," to describe their way of life, which included robbery and theft. For them, to "crip" meant to steal.

As the Crips gang grew during the 1970s, it developed rivalries with other gangs. Since the Crips were well organized, they could call on affiliates during turf wars and other fights. In 1973, however, the Crips' strength was put to the test when two gangs warring with them—the LA Brims and the Piru Street Boys—formed an alliance to fight the Crips. Since this alliance was considered a "blood" alliance—one that would be as strong as the relationships between blood relatives—the new gang was called the "Bloods." Since then, hundreds of deaths have been attributed to the war between the Crips and the Bloods.

Today, the gangs remain rivals, but it is not unusual for them to drop their feuds when dealing drugs. The gangs know there is plenty of money to go around in the drug business, so they tend to respect each other's turf.

Police say notorious Los Angeles street gangs, such as the Crips and Bloods, have taken over the PCP trade on the West Coast.

President Ronald Reagan announces the Campaign Against Drug Abuse, August 1986. In the fall of that year, Reagan signed the Anti-Drug Abuse Act, which set tough punishments for drug users.

drugs faces the same penalty that would be handed down to a big-time narcotics kingpin who controls millions of dollars in drug profits. Although some advocates have questioned the mandatory minimum sentencing guidelines adopted by state and federal courts, the tough drug laws have remained on the books.

Mandatory minimum sentences are only one weapon in the arsenal against narcotics trafficking. In addition, the federal government as well as state governments have adopted laws giving prosecutors the power to seize the assets of people convicted of dealing drugs. Under these laws, people found guilty of dealing PCP will lose not only their freedom, but also their money, homes, cars, and any merchandise that might have been purchased with the proceeds of illegal drug sales. In 1997, the DEA seized more than $500 million in cash, real estate, cars, boats, airplanes, and other assets from drug dealers. That same year, prosecutors on the state and county levels seized more than $700 million in assets from drug dealers.

Targeting Sophisticated Methods

Selling PCP promises enormous profits, so it is rare for big-time drug kingpins to tolerate small-time dealers cutting into their business. Instead, West Coast street gangs have taken over the

PCP trade, distributing the drug in Los Angeles and other western U.S. cities and moving it across the country, where they have struck deals with Midwest and East Coast street gangs to carry on the trade. In one recent case, a member of a gang distributing PCP and cocaine was discovered working as a baggage handler at Los Angeles International Airport. Because of his position, the

Federal Trafficking Penalties for PCP (Schedule II)

Quantity	Penalties
10 to 99 gms pure or 100 to 999 gms mixture	**First offense:** Not less than 5 years and not more than 40 years. If death or serious injury, not less than 20 or more than life. Fine of not more than $2 million if an individual, $5 million if not an individual.
	Second offense: Not less than 10 years, and not more than life. If death or serious injury, life imprisonment. Fine of not more than $4 million if an individual, $10 million if not an individual.

Quantity	Penalties
100 gm or more pure or 1 kg or more mixture	**First offense:** Not less than 10 years, and not more than life. If death or serious injury, not less than 20 or more than life. Fine of not more than $4 million if an individual, $10 million if not an individual.
	Second offense: Not less than 20 years, and not more than life. If death or serious injury, life imprisonment. Fine of not more than $8 million if an individual, $20 million if not an individual.
	2 or more prior offenses: Life imprisonment.

baggage handler was able to circumvent airport security and hide drugs on airliners bound for the East Coast.

Other gangs ship PCP by commercial package carriers, hiding the drugs in bottles that formerly held sports drinks. A DEA report states that "17 of the 24 PCP laboratories seized throughout the United States from 1998 to 2002 were located in California. As they have for decades . . . street gangs, operating primarily in Los Angeles and San Bernardino County, produce most of the

Additional Dangers

Dealers take serious risks just manufacturing PCP, because the process requires the use of highly flammable and toxic chemicals. During the 1970s and 1980s, explosions in basement or backyard drug labs were not uncommon.

At that time, police determined that most PCP labs were located near industrial East Coast cities such as Philadelphia, Baltimore, and Newark because drug makers found it easy to steal the ingredients from local chemical companies in these areas. In a March 24, 1988, article in *Rolling Stone* magazine, written by Tom McNichol, Robert O'Leary, a former undercover agent for the DEA in the Washington-Baltimore area, described a common PCP lab:

> The typical lab setup around here used to be two or three burnouts from the suburbs and their girlfriends holed up in a shack in the woods somewhere between Baltimore and Washington. They'd be driving around for a couple of days, picking up ice buckets and chemicals, and we'd be following them around, hiding in the bushes with binoculars, watching them cook the stuff. We're not talking about rocket scientists here. Some of these kids are pouring out ether to evaporate some of the chemicals while they've got a lit doobie [marijuana cigarette] hanging out of their mouth. When the ether fumes fill up the room—bang! There's a huge flash. I saw that once in Baltimore County. We were out in the woods watching them through binoculars, and there was a big flash from inside the house. They all ran out, gagging and coughing. Then, believe it or not, they went back in after a while and continued to mix."

As that example illustrates, during the 1970s and 1980s, the manufacture of PCP was undertaken primarily by individuals who could cook up a batch in their basements and then sell it to a steady and regular clientele. Once the police knew where to find the basement labs, it was an easy matter to shut down the operations.

PCP available nationwide. These groups typically produce PCP in liquid form and subsequently handle the wholesale distribution of the drug to mid-level distributors in Chicago, Houston, Los Angeles, Milwaukee, New Orleans, Newark, New York City, Philadelphia and Washington, D.C."[63]

Widespread Distribution

Two of the most notorious West Coast gangs working in the PCP trade are the Crips and the Bloods. They have struck alliances with gangs of immigrants, from Belize and other Caribbean nations, who settled in East Coast and Midwestern cities and handle distribution of the drugs. In 1996, New York City police announced the arrests of 119 drug dealers in East Harlem. The ring generated some fifteen thousand dollars in profits daily. Their source of drugs was a single laboratory in southern California.

Once the drugs arrived in New York, they were distributed to eight gangs that operated in the city and sold to customers under various "brand names": Lethal Weapon, Free Willy, Beyond and Back, and Purple Rain, among others. These gangs also made the PCP available to gangs operating in Boston, Philadelphia, Washington, D.C., and other cities. DEA agent Carlo Boccia told a reporter, "They shared a common source of supply, but they operated independently in terms of distribution and customer base."[64]

In late 2004, federal drug agents in Cleveland seized more than one million dollars worth of PCP that was delivered to drug peddlers in a sealed jug. Federal prosecutors said the source of the drug was a Los Angeles-based gang. "This was a major bust," said U.S. attorney Gregory White. "That's a lot of PCP. We have PCP labs in rural areas and in urban settings in northern Ohio. We're trying to root them out with the resources we have."[65] Drug agents were tipped to the delivery by an informant, who led them to the home of a drug dealer named Tyrone Madden. At Madden's home, drug agents found a small quantity of the drug as well as a handgun hidden in a diaper bag. Facing arrest for peddling PCP, Madden agreed to cooperate and turn over a huge supply of the drug that he was expecting to be delivered shortly. Madden made a phone call, and soon a car arrived at his home, driven by a Los Angeles man identified by drug agents as J. T. Carr. In the trunk of Carr's vehicle, drug agents found the jug. The drug agents arrested Carr, who was identified as a member of the Crips.

Certainly, PCP distribution is not confined to the inner-city neighborhoods of Boston, Philadelphia, Cleveland, and New York City. But whether the drug eventually finds its way to the upscale suburb of Greenwich, Connecticut, or rural Lancaster County in Pennsylvania, chances are the PCP was manufactured in a lab hidden deep in a tough urban neighborhood of Southern California.

Becoming Harder to Stop

Authorities have estimated that there may be as many as thirteen hundred gangs based in Los Angeles, most of them affiliated with the Bloods and Crips. Not all of them are in the PCP business, but if they are not dealing phencyclidine, they might be selling marijuana, crack cocaine, or heroin. These gangs are also becoming extremely sophisticated in their methods. In recent years, investigators have found drug dealers turning to technology to grow their illicit trades. In a 2004 report, the White House Office of National Drug Control Policy said throwaway cell phones and the Internet have enabled drug dealers to communicate in ways they could not before.

Authorities do not suggest that PCP is manufactured only in Los Angeles. In recent years the DEA has shut down sizable PCP labs in Connecticut, Indiana, Maryland, Nevada, Oklahoma, and Texas. In 2001, a PCP lab in Gary, Indiana, was shut down, cutting off the supply of phencyclidine for most of Chicago's PCP dealers. In New York City, Newark, and Philadelphia, PCP labs run by outlaw motorcycle gangs have been uncovered and shut down. Since 2000, the DEA conducted raids on gangs in Arizona, Kansas, Missouri, and New Mexico, seizing PCP as well as the raw chemicals used to make the drug. According to a DEA report, "There are indications of a PCP resurgence. Recent large seizures of the drug, coupled with the discovery of clandestine laboratories operating outside of traditional source areas, may be an indication that demand for PCP is increasing. Even though the trafficking and abuse of PCP is not as widespread as with other illicit drugs, the violent consequences of its abuse are always causes for concern."[66]

Fighting PCP City to City

Combating this new wave of PCP trafficking is not easy. For starters, the origin of the PCP trade cannot be traced to other countries, such as Colombia, where most of the supply of cocaine originates, or the border area of Thailand, Myanmar (formerly Burma) and Laos in Asia (the so-called Golden Triangle), which is responsible for producing much of the world's opium. When fighting to curtail the trafficking of those drugs, the United States can sign treaties and other international agreements to enlist allies. What is more, military forces such as the U.S. Navy and Coast Guard can be employed to patrol the oceans, searching for drug-carrying vessels. In 2001, the United States agreed to devote $3.3 billion to "Plan Colombia," to help train and equip Colombian drug agents who investigate that country's widespread cocaine trade. By 2004, Plan Colombia was showing results: drug authorities had wiped out the cocaine crop on some 140,000 acres, and the amount of cocaine seized by authorities had increased sixfold.

PCP, on the other hand, is produced within the United States, using chemicals that are legally available for industrial purposes. Therefore, law enforcement agencies must fight PCP dealers city by city, neighborhood by neighborhood, employing tools familiar to every street cop—undercover investigations, confidential informants, and electronic surveillance.

Typically, a police department or other law enforcement agency, such as the DEA, sends an undercover agent into a neighborhood where drugs are being sold. The agent finds the dealer and asks for drugs. Money changes hands. Other undercover operatives stationed nearby record the transaction, using electronic surveillance equipment such as hidden cameras and microphones. After the drug purchase is made, police move in on the dealer, taking him into custody.

In a typical undercover operation, just before Christmas 2002, two Washington, D.C., police officers working undercover approached a dealer in a neighborhood known for its drug violence. "Gimme two dips,"[67] one of the officers told the dealer, who then retrieved a small vial from a hiding place near some concrete steps. As soon as the dealer produced the PCP, police officers hidden throughout the neighborhood swarmed to the street corner, where they took the drug dealer into custody.

In many such cases, the defendant will be offered a deal if he cooperates: police may agree to drop the charges against him, or they may petition the court for a light sentence, if the dealer agrees to lead them to the lab producing the PCP and to the drug kingpins calling the shots. When drug dealers are faced with mandatory minimum sentences that can send them to jail for years, it is not surprising that many agree to cooperate; some people then refer to them as "snitches," a slang label for people who turn in others.

In an interview for the PBS documentary *Snitch*, convicted drug dealer Ronald Rankins explained why he cooperated with drug agents and turned in his friend:

> I don't care what people think about me . . . they can call me a snitch or whatever they want to call me. But any man faced with those kind of terms . . . he's going to have to weigh his options, you know what I'm saying? And that you're knowing these people to be serious, speaking of the government, in saying that one of you is going to receive a life sentence, you decide who's going to receive it. They're giving me the option to decide who's going to receive the life sentence. I love my life just as much as any man and I don't want to spend the rest of my life in prison. It's just like I didn't want him to spend the rest of his life in prison. But they tricked me and made it easier for me to decide by saying that he was trying to roll me [cooperate with the authorities].[68]

In return for cooperating, Rankins received a fifteen-year jail term for drug dealing, and a promise of reduced time if he continued to provide police with information about the illegal drug trade.

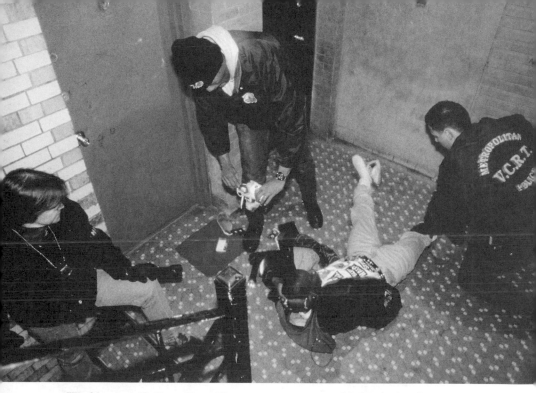

Washington, D.C., police officers arrest a suspected PCP dealer during a drug raid in a public housing building.

Strategies for Prevention

The police get involved only after PCP is already in the neighborhood. Clearly schools, community groups, and parents have a responsibility to convince young people to stay away from the drug. In America today, there are dozens of highly-effective drug prevention programs that have been established by schools and local groups as well as national organizations. They are targeted at children of all ages, from the preschool level through high school. Many of them send direct messages about drug abuse. For example, the Partnership for a Drug-Free America receives free space in newspapers, magazines, and other publications and free air time on national TV broadcasts to provide antidrug advertising and other programming aimed at young people. In 2004, the partnership aired campaigns against marijuana and methamphetamine use. Also that year, athletes participating in the Gravity Games, which were telecast on the Outdoor Life Network, agreed to tape antidrug messages that were aired during the telecasts. Officials

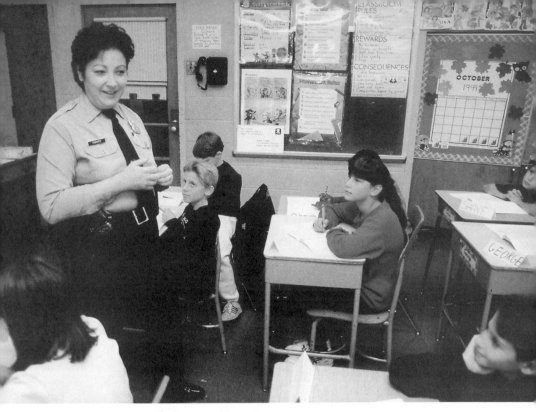

In many schools police officers teach young people about the dangers of PCP and other drugs through the DARE (Drug Abuse Resistance Education) program.

from the partnership believed the Gravity Games provided an ideal venue to reach the type of young people who could be most influenced by antidrug messages. Said partnership vice president Stan Weil, "This is a wonderful opportunity for the Partnership to reach 160,000 of our target audience—sensation-seeking, at-risk teens—with our messages."[69] Meanwhile in 2004, Comcast, the cable TV company, worked with the partnership to sponsor town meetings in Detroit, Miami, and Boston that focused on antidrug messages. Comcast broadcast the town meetings over its cable network.

Other prevention programs try to reach out directly to teen drug users or teens at risk. Sometimes, these programs do not provide a specific antidrug message; rather, they try to provide young people with the cognitive skills that help them make their own decisions about whether to use drugs. According to the National Institute on Drug Abuse, some of the leading prevention programs in America include Caring School Community Program, which focuses on convincing young people to become more dedicated to their schoolwork and other school-based activities, and the Lions-Quest Skills for Adolescence program, which concentrates on building self-esteem in young people and teaching them personal responsibility, communication, and decision-making skills. Another program praised by the federal government is Project Alert, which is presented to students in their classrooms. Under Project Alert, teachers lead discussions in small groups that challenge the myths students may have about drug use.

A similar program is known as the Project Towards No Drug Abuse, which is aimed at young people between the ages of fourteen and nineteen. The Project Towards No Drug Abuse also seeks to challenge the myths many teens may harbor about whether drugs are truly bad for them. In California, the program tries to reach youths who are believed to be most at risk to use drugs or are already using drugs.

Under the program, students attend nine classroom sessions over the course of three weeks. Students are asked to play roles, asking themselves hard questions while setting goals for themselves. In one role-playing game, the students are asked to fight against the stereotype of themselves—that they are drug-abusing loafers with no goals in life. Says Dr. Steven Sussman, the University of Southern California psychologist who developed the program, "What we're doing in nine lessons is trying to find motivators for change that are personally relevant for these high-risk youths. Basically, we are getting them to be more internally and externally consistent so their behavior matches what they think of themselves and what they want."[70]

Parents Play a Key Role

Experts believe, though, that the most effective measures for preventing the abuse of PCP and other drugs start at home. In its report *Preventing Drug Use Among Children and Adolescents*, the National Institute on Drug Abuse says parents should take the time to talk to their children about the dangers of using drugs.

"Family-based prevention programs should enhance family bonding and relationships and include parenting skills; practice in developing, discussing and enforcing family policies on substance abuse; and training in drug education and information," says the report. "Family bonding is the bedrock of the relationship between parents and children."[71]

Growing Threat

Although PCP is certainly a drug of concern that is addressed by many prevention programs, it is believed that few prevention measures are aimed specifically at phencyclidine abuse. And there is no question that despite the growing threat of PCP, federal drug authorities have not developed a national strategy to combat the sale and use of the drug. Without a strategy formulated specifically to wipe out the PCP trade in America, police will continue to pursue the drug dealers on the street corners, then work their way up to the gang leaders who run the laboratories and distribution networks. Meanwhile, schools and human services agencies will educate young people about the horrors of the drug and hope that young people get the message.

As for people who have already tried the drug and decide to go back for more, until medical science develops a way to block the drug's addictive qualities, these users will find themselves facing a long and tortured road when they are ready to quit. Today's PCP users must suffer the effects of their drug of choice—hallucinations, delusions, and violent behavior. In the meantime, society remains burdened with the terrible and unpredictable consequences of people addicted to a truly monstrous drug.

Notes

Introduction: PCP: An American Tragedy

1. Quoted in David A. Fahrenthold, "Use of PCP Rebounding in DC Area; Violence Follows Rise in Drug's Popularity," *Washington Post*, January 5, 2003, p. C-1.
2. Shalia K. Dewan, "A Drug Feared in the '70s Is Tied to Suspect in Killings," *New York Times*, April 6, 2003, p. A-31.
3. Danielle Ompad and David Vlahov, "PCP Use in New York," *New York Times*, April 11, 2003, p. A-24.
4. *Drug Situation in Canada—2003*, Criminal Intelligence Directorate, Royal Canadian Mounted Police, July 2004.

Chapter 1: Good Intentions Go Awry

5. Harvey W. Feldman, "PCP Use in Four Cities: An Overview," *Angel Dust: An Ethnographic Study of PCP Users*, Lexington, Mass.: Lexington Books, 1979, p. 38.
6. George M. Beschner and Harvey W. Feldman, "Introduction," *Angel Dust: An Ethnographic Study of PCP Users*, pp. 8–9.
7. Beschner and Feldman, "Introduction," p 9.
8. Quoted in Dawn MacKeen, "Kicking the PCP Habit," Salon.com, August 24, 1999.
9. Robert C. Petersen and Richard C. Stillman, "Phencyclidine: An Overview," *Phencyclidine Abuse: An Appraisal*. Rockville, Maryland: National Institute on Drug Abuse, August 1978, p. 5.
10. James M. Walters, "Buzzin: PCP Use in Philadelphia," *Angel Dust: An Ethnographic Study of PCP Users*, p. 85.
11. John Newmeyer and Gregory Johnson, "Drug Emergencies in Crowds: An Analysis of Rock Medicine, 1973–1977," *Control Over Intoxicant Use: Pharmacologi-*

cal, Psychological and Social Considerations. New York: Human Sciences Press, 1982, pp. 127–137.

12. Newmeyer and Johnson, "Drug Emergencies in Crowds," p. 133.

13. Quoted in William L. Chaze, "The Deadly Path of Today's PCP Epidemic," *U.S. News and World Report*, November 19, 1984, p. 65.

14. Quoted in Jennifer James and Elena Andresen, "Sea-Tac and PCP," *Angel Dust: An Ethnographic Study of PCP Users*, p. 143.

15. Quoted in James and Andresen, "Sea-Tac and PCP," p. 127.

16. Quoted in Suzanne Smalley and Debra Rosenberg, "I Felt Like I Wanted to Hurt People," *Newsweek*, July 22, 2002, p. 32.

17. Judy Ball, Tracy Garfield, Carol Morin, and Diane Steele, *Emergency Department Trends from the Drug Abuse Warning Network, Final Estimates 1995–2002.* Washington, D.C.: U.S. Department of Health and Human Services, July 2003, p. 104.

18. Quoted in Jennifer Golz, "Lollipops Filled with Illegal Drugs Circulate Chicago Streets," *Columbia Chronicle*, March 15, 2004.

19. Quoted in Smalley and Rosenberg, "I Felt Like I Wanted to Hurt People," p. 32.

Chapter 2: How PCP Affects the Brain

20. Quoted in Ronald K. Siegel, "Phencyclidine and Ketamine Intoxication: A Study of Four Populations of Recreational Users," *Phencyclidine Abuse: An Appraisal.* Rockville, Maryland: National Institute on Drug Abuse, August 1978, p. 122.

21. Quoted in Siegel, "Phencyclidine and Ketamine Intoxication: A Study of Four Populations of Recreational Users," p. 121.

22. Quoted in James and Andresen, "Sea-Tac and PCP," p. 136.

23. Quoted in James and Andresen, "Sea-Tac and PCP," p. 137.

24. Judy Howard, Leila Beckwith, and Carol Rodning, "Adaptive Behavior in Recovering Female Phencyclidine/Polysubstance Abusers," *Residual Effects of Abused Drugs on Behavior Research*. Rockville, Maryland: National Institute on Drug Abuse, 1990, p. 90.

25. Quoted in Tom McNichol, "PCP: The Cheap Thrill With a High Price," *Rolling Stone*, March 24, 1988, p. 85.

26. Quoted in McNichol, "PCP: The Cheap Thrill With a High Price," p. 173.

27. Feldman, "PCP Use in Four Cities: An Overview," p. 43.

28. Quoted in W. Wayne Wiebel, "Burning Out on the Northwest Side: PCP Use in Chicago," *Angel Dust: An Ethnographic Study of PCP Users*, p. 174.

29. Quoted in McNichol, "PCP: The Cheap Thrill With a High Price," p. 84.

30. Quoted in McNichol, "PCP: The Cheap Thrill With a High Price," p. 84.

31. Quoted in McNichol, "PCP: The Cheap Thrill With a High Price," p. 85.

32. Quoted in Siegel, "Phencyclidine and Ketamine Intoxication," p. 124.

33. Steven E. Lerner and R. Stanley Burns, "Phencyclidine Use Among Youth: History, Epidemiology, and Acute Chronic Intoxication," *Phencyclidine Abuse: An Appraisal*. Rockville, Maryland: National Institute on Drug Abuse, August 1978, p. 93.

34. Lerner and Burns, "Phencyclidine Use Among Youth: History, Epidemiology, and Acute Chronic Intoxication," p. 93.

35. Quoted in James and Andresen, "Sea-Tac and PCP," pp. 146–47.

Chapter 3: The Physical Effects of PCP

36. Quoted in Nik Bonopartis, "Angel Dust Use on Upswing in Valley," *Poughkeepsie Journal*, July 5, 2004.
37. Quoted in Hal Marcovitz, "Sellersville Man Sentenced in Assaults—Drug Made 19-year-old Feel Like 'Superman,' Attorney Says," *Allentown Morning Call*, October 16, 2002, p. B-1.
38. Quoted in Peggy O'Hare, Dale Lezon, and Lise Olsen, "Wrong-way Driver Took Drugs, Tests Find; PCP, Ecstasy, Marijuana Used Before Fatal Collision," *Houston Chronicle*, September 11, 2003, p. A-15.
39. Quoted in Alice McQuillan and Michele McPhee, "Cops Nab Brooklyn 'Thrill Killer,'" *New York Daily News*, March 30, 2003, p. 3.
40. Quoted in Heather Hollingsworth, "Man Convicted of Killing Three Sentenced to Life in Prison," Associated Press, September 3, 2004.
41. Quoted in Siegel, "Phencyclidine and Ketamine Intoxication," p. 123.
42. McNichol, "PCP: The Cheap Thrill With a High Price," p. 82.
43. Quoted in Timothy W. Maier, "PCP Is Rearing Its Ugly Head Again," *Insight on the News*, February 4, 2003.
44. Quoted in Andrea Siegel, "Teen Gets 30 Years for Killing," *Baltimore Sun*, August 5, 2004, p. 1.
45. Quoted in Michael Goldberg, "James Brown Addicted to PCP," *Rolling Stone*, November 17, 1988, p. 42.
46. Quoted in Goldberg, "James Brown Addicted to PCP," p. 42.
47. Quoted in "James Brown's Wife Died After Taking PCP and Prescription Drugs, Autopsy Report Says," *Jet*, February 26, 1996, p. 18.
48. Quoted in Michael Goldberg, "Wrestling with the Devil: The Struggle for the Soul of James Brown," *Rolling Stone*, April 6, 1989, p. 36.

49. "Operation Running Waters Leads to Major PCP Arrests,"
    U.S. Drug Enforcement Administration news release, September 4, 2003. http://www.usdoj.gov/dea/pubs/states
    /newsrel/la090403.html
50. "California Man Sentenced for Environmental and Drug
    Crimes," U.S. Environmental Protection Agency news release, November 15, 1996.

Chapter 4: Coming Down from the High

51. Quoted in Joann Loviglio, "All Wet, Dangerous New
    High: Kids Use Embalming Fluid as Recreational Drug,"
    Associated Press, July 27, 2003.
52. Quoted in McNichol, "PCP: The Cheap Thrill With a
    High Price," p. 173.
53. David A. Gorelick, "Outpatient Treatment of PCP Users,"
    American Journal of Drug and Alcohol Abuse, December
    1989, p. 322.
54. David A. Gorelick, "Outpatient Treatment of PCP Users,"
    p. 326.
55. Feldman, "PCP Use in Four Cities: An Overview," p. 43.
56. Gorelick, "Outpatient Treatment of PCP Users," p. 326.
57. Gerald G. DeAngelis and Elliott Goldstein, "Long Term
    Treatment of Adolescent PCP Abusers," *Phencyclidine
    Abuse: An Appraisal*. Rockville, Maryland: National Institute on Drug Abuse, August 1978, p. 269.
58. DeAngelis and Goldstein, "Long Term Treatment of Adolescent PCP Abusers," p. 268.
59. Quoted in MacKeen, "Kicking the PCP Habit."
60. Quoted in Eric Hand, "Tobacco Plays Role in Study of
    Abuse," *Arkansas Democrat-Gazette*, August 1, 2004, p.
    B-1.

Chapter 5: The War on PCP

61. Quoted in Greg Krikorian, "16 Accused of Making, Selling PCP," *Los Angeles Times*, July 31, 1997, p. 3.

62. *PCP: The Threat Remains* (DEA Drug Intelligence Brief). Alexandria, Virginia: U.S. Drug Enforcement Administration, May 2003. www.usdoj.gov/dea/pubs/intel/03013/03013.pdf

63. Quoted in McNichol, "PCP: The Cheap Thrill With a High Price," p. 82.

64. Quoted in Mae M. Cheng, "PCP: That Old Devil Angel Dust Makes a Comeback on Streets," *Newsday*, April 12, 1996, p. 8.

65. Quoted in John Caniglia, "Drug Agents Seize PCP in 'Major Bust' in Cleveland," *Cleveland Plain Dealer*, Oct. 23, 2004, p. B-1.

66. *PCP: The Threat Remains.* www.usdoj.gov/dea/pubs/intel/03013/03013.pdf

67. Quoted in Fahrenthold, "Use of PCP Rebounding in DC Area."

68. "Inside the Mind of a Snitch," transcript from the PBS Frontline documentary *Snitch*, January 1999. www.pbs.org/wgbh/pages/frontline/shows/snitch/etc/rankins.html.

69. Quoted in "Partnership for a Drug-Free America to Partner With Outdoor Life Network to Reach Teens at Gravity Games," www.drugfreeamerica.com

70. Quoted in Robert Mathias, *National Institute on Drug Abuse Notes*, May-June 2003, p. 10.

71. *Preventing Drug Use Among Children and Adolescents.* Bethesda, Md.: National Institute on Drug Abuse, 2003. http://www.nida.nih.gov/Prevention/Prevopen.html

Organizations
to Contact

Centers for Disease Control and Prevention
Office of Communication
Building 16, D-42
1600 Clifton Road, N.E.
Atlanta, GA 30333
(800) 311-3435
www.cdc.gov

The federal government's public health agency charts risky behavior by young people through the Youth Risk Behavior Surveillance System. Reports from the surveillance system can be downloaded through the CDC's website. The reports chart drug and alcohol use as well as other risky behavior by young people, including sex and smoking.

Drug Enforcement Administration
2401 Jefferson Davis Highway
Alexandria, VA 22301
(202) 307-1000
www.usdoj.gov/dea

The U.S. Justice Department's chief antidrug law enforcement agency is charged with investigating the illegal narcotics trade in the United States and with helping local police agencies with their antidrug efforts. The agency maintains 237 field offices in the United States as well as 58 offices in foreign countries. Visitors to the agency's website will find statistics, news releases, photographs, and a state-by-state analysis of the illegal narcotics trade.

National Drug Intelligence Center
319 Washington Street, 5th Floor
Johnstown, PA 15901-1622
(814) 532-4601
www.usdoj.gov/ndic

A division within the Justice Department, the agency provides intelligence on drug trends to government leaders and law enforcement agencies and produces the National Drug Threat Assessment, which identifies the primary drugs that have invaded illegal markets, tracks their availability in American communities, monitors fluctuations in drug use, and analyzes drug trafficking patterns.

National Health Information Center
Referral Specialist
P.O. Box 1133
Washington, DC 20013-1133
(800) 336-4797
www.health.gov/NHIC

The National Health Information Center helps people with questions about health issues contact an appropriate government agency or social services program. By using the agency's website, people can search a database for an agency or organization that may help them get the information they need. NHIC also produces three annual health information directories: *Federal Health Information Centers and Clearinghouses*, *National Health Observances*, and *Toll-free Numbers for Health Information*.

National Institute on Alcohol Abuse and Alcoholism
5635 Fishers Lane, MSC 9304
Bethesda, Maryland 20892-9304
(800) 662-HELP
Website: www.niaaa.nih.gov/other/referral.htm

While the National Institute on Alcohol Abuse and Alcoholism is primarily focused on developing treatment and prevention programs for alcohol abuse, the agency does maintain a substance abuse treatment facility locator that will provide information on drug treatment to people who call a toll-free number. Callers can obtain printed materials on alcohol and drug information, as well as the locations of substance abuse treatment centers near their homes.

National Institute on Drug Abuse
6001 Executive Boulevard, Room 5213
Bethesda, MD 20892-9561
(301) 443-1124
Website: www.nida.nih.gov

Part of the National Institutes of Health, the NIDA's mission is to help finance scientific research projects that study addiction trends and treatment of chronic drug users. The agency's website features many links for young people, including a "Back to School" site that provides students with scientific information about drug abuse, and the "Mind Over Matter" link, which explains to teens how the brain reacts to different drugs, including hallucinogens, marijuana, steroids, nicotine, and inhalants.

National Library of Medicine
8600 Rockville Pike
Bethesda, MD 20894
(888) 346-3656
Website: dirline.nlm.nih.gov

The National Library of Medicine serves as the medical library for the National Institutes of Health. The library's collection includes more than seven million books, journals, technical reports, manuscripts, microfilms, photographs, and images, covering medical and health-related fields. Visitors to the library's website will find the Directory of Health Organizations Online, which helps people find organizations and agencies that can answer their health-related questions. A search for groups devoted to drug addiction issues turned up eighty-one entries.

Partnership for a Drug-Free America
405 Lexington Avenue, Suite 1601
New York, NY 10174
(212) 922-1560.
www.drugfreeamerica.org

Funded by American corporations and media organizations that provide free advertising space, the partnership helps convince young people to stay away from drugs. On the organization's website, young visitors will find articles on talking to friends about drug use, how to recognize if drug or alcohol use is out of control, and testimonials from young people about their drug habits and how they kicked them. Teens can leave messages about friends and family members who died from drug abuse on the website's "Memorial Wall."

Substance Abuse and Mental Health Services Administration
1 Choke Cherry Road
Room 8-1054
Rockville, MD 20857
(240) 276-2000
www.samhsa.gov

An agency of the U.S. Department of Health and Human Services, the Substance Abuse and Mental Health Services Administration (SAMHSA) helps develop programs for people who are at risk for becoming drug abusers. Visitors to the agency's website can find information on many treatment and prevention programs designed for substance abusers, as well as updates on the agency's efforts to help prison inmates free themselves of their drug habits. Young people can find information on SAMHSA's Safe and Drug-Free Schools programs. Also, reports by the Drug Abuse Warning Network (DAWN) can be downloaded through the SAMHSA web page. SAMHSA also provides a substance abuse treatment facility locator through the link at http://findtreatment.samhsa.gov. Visitors can use the locater to search for a nearby drug treatment program; more than 11,000 are listed in SAMHSA's database.

White House Office of National Drug Control Policy
Drug Policy Information Clearinghouse
PO Box 6000
Rockville, MD 20849-6000
(800) 666-3332
www.whitehousedrugpolicy.gov

The White House Office of National Drug Control Policy was established to develop a national strategy to combat illegal drug use. The office serves as a liaison serving the different federal drug investigation and research agencies and helps provide information to state and local agencies that fight drug abuse. The president's national drug strategy can be downloaded at the office's website, which is maintained by the White House. Other reports on substance abuse trends are available as well. Teens may check out the link for the "Media Campaign," which features several activities for young people, including the "Steer Clear of Pot" program, aimed at new drivers, and the "Group Activity Guide," which suggests several ways students can become involved in antidrug activities.

For Further Reading

James Barter, *Hallucinogens*. San Diego, California: Lucent Books, 2002. General overview of hallucinogenic drugs, with information about their use from ancient times to the present.

Marilyn Carroll, *PCP: The Dangerous Angel*. Philadelphia: Chelsea House Publishers, 1992. Discusses a wide range of issues associated with phencyclidine abuse, including dependence on the drug and treatment of users.

Jennifer Croft, *PCP: High Risk on the Streets*. New York: Rosen Publishing Group, 1998. Includes many stories of PCP users describing the experiences and consequences of taking the drug.

Gerald Newman and Eleanor Newman Layfield, *PCP*. Springfield, New Jersey: Enslow Publishers Inc., 1997. History of the drug, its effects on the body, and impact on society are among the topics covered.

Jane Ellen Phillips, *LSD, PCP, and Other Hallucinogens*. Philadelphia: Chelsea House Publishers, 2000. Basic information on the abuse and effects of PCP, LSD, ketamine, and other hallucinogenic drugs, including such obscure substances as bufotenine, which is secreted by toads.

Paul R. Robbins, *Hallucinogens*. Springfield, New Jersey: Enslow Publishers, 1996. Provides a background on many hallucinogenic drugs, including LSD, PCP, peyote, mescaline, and magic mushrooms.

Works Consulted

Books

Harvey W. Feldman, Michael H. Agar, and George M. Beschner, editors. *Angel Dust: An Ethnographic Study of PCP Users.* Lexington, Mass.: Lexington Books, 1979. Contains studies of PCP abuse in the cities of Philadelphia, Miami, Chicago, and Seattle and Tacoma, Washington.

James N. Parker and Philip M. Parker, eds., *The Official Patient's Sourcebook on PCP Dependence.* San Diego, California: ICON Health Publications, 2002. Describes addiction therapies available for people with PCP habits and provides resources, many of which are Internet-based, where more information is available.

Robert C. Petersen and Richard C. Stillman, eds., *Phencyclidine Abuse: An Appraisal, National Institute on Drug Abuse Research* Monograph 21. Rockville, Maryland: National Institute on Drug Abuse, August 1978. Comprehensive study of phencyclidine and its effects on the brains and bodies of its users.

Solomon H. Snyder, *Drugs and the Brain.* New York: Scientific American Library, 1986. Describes the physiological changes that take place in the brain due to drug abuse.

John W. Spencer and John J. Boren, eds., *Residual Effects of Abused Drugs on Behavior Research, National Institute on Drug Abuse Research* Monograph 101. Rockville, Maryland: National Institute on Drug Abuse, 1990. Includes a chapter by Judy Howard, Leila Beckwith, and Carol Rodning titled

"Adaptive Behavior in Recovering Female Phencyclidine/Poly-substance Abusers," which examines PCP's effects on babies born to PCP-addicted mothers.

Norman E. Zinberg and Wayne M. Harding, *Control Over Intoxicant Use: Pharmacological, Psychological and Social Considerations*. New York: Human Sciences Press, 1982. Contains an essay by John Newmeyer and Gregory Johnson on PCP use observed at the Haight-Ashbury Free Medical Clinic; other essays explore abuse of LSD and heroin as well as the social reasons behind people's decisions to abuse drugs.

Periodicals

"Aspiring Rapper who Killed Roommate and Ate Her Lung Sentenced to Life," *Associated Press*, November 8, 2003.

Nik Bonopartis, "Angel Dust Use on Upswing in Valley," *Poughkeepsie Journal*, July 5, 2004.

Kathy Braidhill, "Where the Boyz Are: Gang Activity in Los Angeles Metropolitan Area," *Los Angeles Magazine*, January 1998.

"California Man Sentenced for Environmental and Drug Crimes," U.S. Environmental Protection Agency news release, November 15, 1996.

Tom Cahill, "Moonwalk Serenade: On Story Road, in the Heart of the Barrio, a Lowride's a Slow Ride, PCP is Called KJ, and Brain Cells Burn at Night," *Rolling Stone*, July 13, 1978.

John Caniglia, "Drug Agents Seize PCP in 'Major Bust' in Cleveland," *Cleveland Plain-Dealer*, October 23, 2004.

Matthew Cella, "PCP Rivals Use of Crack in District; Rise in Homicides Linked to Its Abuse," *Washington Times*, December 14, 2002.

William L. Chaze, "The Deadly Path of Today's PCP Epidemic," *U.S. News and World Report*, November 19, 1984.

Mae M. Cheng, "PCP: That Old Devil Angel Dust Makes a Comeback on Streets," *Newsday*, April 12, 1996.

Shalia K. Dewan, "A Drug Feared in the '70s Is Tied to Suspect in Killings," *New York Times*, April 6, 2003.

David A. Fahrenthold, "Use of PCP Rebounding in DC Area; Violence Follows Rise in Drug's Popularity," *Washington Post*, January 5, 2003.

Michael Goldberg, "James Brown Addicted to PCP," *Rolling Stone*, November 17, 1988.

Michael Goldberg, "Wrestling with the Devil: The Struggle for the Soul of James Brown," *Rolling Stone*, April 6, 1989.

Jennifer Golz, "Lollipops Filled with Illegal Drugs Circulate Chicago Streets," *Columbia Chronicle*, March 15, 2004.

Eric Hand, "Tobacco Plays Role in Study of Abuse," *Arkansas Democrat-Gazette*, August 1, 2004.

Valerie Hickey, "Officers Are Shocked at Taser's Power," *The News-Herald*, October 2, 2004.

Heather Hollingsworth, "Man Convicted of Killing Three Sentenced to Life in Prison," Associated Press, September 3, 2004.

John Horton, "Kids Find They Can Start High at a Store: Teens Abusing Medications," *Cleveland Plain Dealer*, September 27, 2004.

"James Brown's Wife Died After Taking PCP and Prescription Drugs, Autopsy Report Says," *Jet*, February 26, 1996.

Joann Loviglio, "All Wet, Dangerous New High: Kids Use Embalming Fluid as Recreational Drug," Associated Press, July 27, 2003.

Greg Krikorian, "16 Accused of Making, Selling PCP," *Los Angeles Times*, July 31, 1997.

Timothy W. Maier, "PCP Is Rearing Its Ugly Head Again," *Insight on the News*, February 4, 2003.

"Man Caught with Pants Down Falls and Can't Get Up," *Lufkin Daily News*, December 12, 2004.

Hal Marcovitz, "Sellersville Man Sentenced in Assaults—Drug Made 19-year-old Feel Like 'Superman,' Attorney Says," *Allentown Morning Call*, October 16, 2002.

Robert Mathias, *National Institute on Drug Abuse Notes*, May-June 2003.

Tom McNichol, "PCP: The Cheap Thrill With a High Price," *Rolling Stone*, March 24, 1988.

Alice McQuillan and Michele McPhee, "Cops Nab Brooklyn 'Thrill Killer,'" *New York Daily News*, March 30, 2003.

Peggy O'Hare, Dale Lezon, and Lise Olsen, "Wrong Way Driver Took Drugs, Tests Find; PCP, Ecstasy, Marijuana Used Before Fatal Collision," *Houston Chronicle*, September 11, 2003.

Danielle Ompad and David Vlahov, "PCP Use in New York," *New York Times*, April 11, 2003.

"Operation Running Waters Leads to Major PCP Arrests," U.S. Drug Enforcement Administration news release, September 4, 2003.

"Outpatient Treatment of PCP Users," *American Journal of Drug and Alcohol Abuse*, December 1989.

Andrea Siegel, "Teen Gets 30 Years for Killing," *Baltimore Sun*, August 5, 2004.

Suzanne Smalley and Debra Rosenberg, "I Felt Like I Wanted to Hurt People," *Newsweek*, July 22, 2002.

Internet Sources

Dawn MacKeen, "Kicking the PCP Habit," August 24, 1999. www.salon.com/health/log/1999/08/24/pcp.html

"Inside the Mind of a Snitch," transcript from the PBS Frontline documentary *Snitch*. www.pbs.org/wgbh/pages/frontline/shows/snitch/etc/rankins.html

Drugs and Human Performance Fact Sheets. National Highway Traffic Safety Administration. www.nhtsa.dot.gov/people/injury/research/job185drugs/

Drug Situation in Canada—2003. Royal Canadian Mounted Police. www.rcmp-grc.gc.ca/crimint/article_e.htm

National Institute on Drug Abuse, *Preventing Drug Use Among Children and Adolescents*. 2003. www.nida.nih.gov/Prevention/Prevopen.html

U.S. Department of Health and Human Services Office of Applied Studies, *Emergency Department Trends from the Drug*

Abuse Warning Network, Final Estimates 1995–2002. July 2003. http://dawninfo.samhsa.gov/old_dawn/pubs_94_02/edpubs/2002final/

U.S. Drug Enforcement Administration, *PCP: The Threat Remains*. May 2003. www.usdoj.gov/dea/pubs/intel/030 13/03013.pdf

University of Michigan, *Monitoring the Future*. 2005. www.monitoringthefuture.org.

Index

Picture Credits

About the Author

Hal Marcovitz is a journalist who lives in Chalfont, Pennsylvania, with his wife, Gail, and daughters Michelle and Ashley. He has written more than sixty books for young readers.